THE GODFATHER IN PICTURES

THE GODFATHER IN PICTURES
AN UNOFFICIAL COMPANION

TONY NOURMAND

Art Direction and Design by Graham Marsh

For Iradj

First published 2007 by Boxtree
an imprint of Pan Macmillan Ltd
Pan Macmillan, 20 New Wharf Road, London N1 9RR
Basingstoke and Oxford
Associated companies throughout the world
www.panmacmillan.com

ISBN 978-0-7522-2637-8

Compiled and edited by Tony Nourmand
Text by Alison Aitchison and Tony Nourmand
Research and co-ordination by Alison Aitchison
Art direction and design by Graham Marsh
Page layouts by Joakim Olsson
Picture research by Rebecca McClelland

9 8 7 6 5 4 3 2 1

A CIP catalogue record for this book is available from
the British Library.

Printed by Butler and Tanner, Somerset

Visit www.panmacmillan.com to read more about all our books and
to buy them. You will also find features, author interviews and news
of any author events, and you can sign up for e-newsletters so that
you're always first to hear about our new releases.

CONTENTS

THE GODFATHER (1972)

Starring

Don Vito Corleone	**MARLON BRANDO**
Michael Corleone	**AL PACINO**
Sonny Corleone	**JAMES CAAN**
Fredo Corleone	**JOHN CAZALE**
Tom Hagen	**ROBERT DUVALL**
Kay Adams	**DIANE KEATON**
Directed by	**FRANCIS FORD COPPOLA**
Original Screenplay by	**MARIO PUZO AND FRANCIS FORD COPPOLA (BASED ON THE BOOK 'THE GODFATHER' BY MARIO PUZO)**
Produced by	**ALBERT S. RUDDY**
Cinematography by	**GORDON WILLIS**
Production Design by	**DEAN TAVOULARIS**
Music by	**NINO ROTA**
Casting by	**FRED ROOS**
Make-up by	**DICK SMITH**
Costume Design by	**ANNA HILL JOHNSTONE**
Edited by	**WILLIAM REYNOLDS & PETER ZINNER**

ACADEMY AWARD NOMINATIONS

FRANCIS FORD COPPOLA
Best Director

JAMES CAAN
Best Actor in a Supporting Role

ROBERT DUVALL
Best Actor in a Supporting Role

AL PACINO
Best Actor in a Supporting Role

ANNA HILL JOHNSTONE
Best Costume Design

WILLIAM REYNOLDS & PETER ZINNER
Best Film Editing

NINO ROTA
Best Music / Original Dramatic Score

CHARLES GRENZBACH, RICHARD PORTMAN & CHRISTOPHER NEWMAN
Best Sound

ACADEMY AWARDS WON

MARLON BRANDO
Best Actor in a Leading Role

ALBERT S. RUDDY
Best Picture

MARIO PUZO & FRANCIS FORD COPPOLA
Best Writing, Screenplay Based on Material from Another Medium.

THE GODFATHER: PART II (1974)

Starring

Don Michael Corleone	**AL PACINO**
Young Vito Corleone	**ROBERT DE NIRO**
Fredo Corleone	**JOHN CAZALE**
Tom Hagen	**ROBERT DUVALL**
Kay Adams	**DIANE KEATON**
Directed by	**FRANCIS FORD COPPOLA**
Original Screenplay by	**MARIO PUZO AND FRANCIS FORD COPPOLA**
	(BASED ON THE BOOK 'THE GODFATHER'
	BY MARIO PUZO)
Produced by	**FRANCIS FORD COPPOLA**
Co-produced by	**FRED ROOS & GRAY FREDERICKSON**
Cinematography by	**GORDON WILLIS**
Production Design by	**DEAN TAVOULARIS**
Music by	**NINO ROTA**
Additional Music by	**CARMINE COPPOLA**
Make-up by	**DICK SMITH**
Costume Design by	**THEADORA VAN RUNKLE**
Edited by	**BARRY MALKIN, RICHARD MARKS**
	AND PETER ZINNER

ACADEMY AWARD NOMINATIONS
AL PACINO
Best Actor in a Leading Role
MICHAEL V. GAZZO
Best Actor in a Supporting Role
LEE STRASBERG
Best Actor in a Supporting Role
TALIA SHIRE
Best Actress in a Supporting Role
THEADORA VAN RUNKLE
Best Costume Design

ACAMEDY AWARDS WON
ROBERT DE NIRO
Best Actor in a Supporting Role
FRANCIS FORD COPPOLA
Best Director
FRANCIS FORD COPPOLA, FRED ROOS & GRAY FREDERICKSON
Best Picture
FRANCIS FORD COPPOLA & MARIO PUZO
Best Writing, Screenplay Adapted From Other Material
NINO ROTA & CARMINE COPPOLA
Best Music / Original Dramatic Score
DEAN TAVOULARIS, ANGELO P. GRAHAM & GEORGE R. NELSON
Best Art Direction-Set Decoration

THE GODFATHER: PART III (1990)

Starring

Don Michael Corleone	**AL PACINO**
Vincent Mancini	**ANDY GARCIA**
Kay Adams	**DIANE KEATON**
Connie Corleone	**TALIA SHIRE**
Mary Corleone	**SOFIA COPPOLA**
Joey Zasa	**JOE MANTEGNA**

Directed by	**FRANCIS FORD COPPOLA**
Original Screenplay by	**MARIO PUZO AND FRANCIS FORD COPPOLA**
Produced by	**FRANCIS FORD COPPOLA**
Co-produced by	**FRED ROOS, GRAY FREDERICKSON AND CHARLES MULVEHILL**
Cinematography by	**GORDON WILLIS**
Production Design by	**DEAN TAVOULARIS**
Music by	**CARMINE COPPOLA**
Costume Design by	**MILENA CANONERO**
Edited by	**BARRY MALKIN, WALTER MURCH AND LISA FRUCHTMAN**

ACADEMY AWARD NOMINATIONS

FRANCIS FORD COPPOLA

Best Picture

ANDY GARCIA

Best Actor in a Supporting Role

FRANCIS FORD COPPOLA

Best Director

GORDON WILLIS

Best Cinematography

DEAN TAVOULARIS & GARY FETTIS

Best Art Direction-Set Decoration

BARRY MALKIN, WALTER MURCH & LISA FRUCHTMAN

Best Film Editing

CARMINE COPPOLA (Music) & **JOHN BETTIS** (Lyrics)

Best Music, Original Song

REVIEWS

THE GODFATHER

"One of the most brutal and moving chronicles of American life ever designed within the limits of popular entertainment." *New York Times*

"What more could we possibly want from a movie?" *Life*

"An Italian-American Gone With the Wind." *Time*

THE GODFATHER: PART II

"The sensibility at work in this film is that of a major artist." *The New Yorker*

"Outstanding in all respects." *Variety*

"A richly detailed, intelligent film that uses overorganized crime as a metaphor to comment on the coldness and corruption of an overorganized modern world." *Time*

THE GODFATHER: PART III

"The Godfather: Part III [is] ...more...mournfully operatic that its predecessors, is as haunted as a film about living characters can be." *New York Times*

"The Godfather: Part III matches its predecessors in narrative intensity, epic scope, socio-political analysis, physical beauty and deep feeling for its characters and milieu." *Variety*

INTRODUCTION

Opposite: Dated 23 January (circa 1970) on headed stationery and written in Puzo's hand:

Dear Mr Brando, I wrote a book called THE GODFATHER which has had some success and I think you're the only actor who can play the ~~part~~ *Godfather with that quiet force and irony the part requires. I hope you'll read the book and like it well enough to use whatever power you can to get the role. I'm writing Paramount to the same effect for whatever good that will do. I know this was presumptuous of me but the best I can do by the role is try. I really think you'd be tremendous. Needless to say I've been an admirer of your art ... Mario Puzo.*

It has been thirty-five years since the release of the first *Godfather* film and more than fifteen years since the last instalment hit movie theatres in 1991, yet the impact of the trilogy and interest surrounding the films shows no sign of abating. Indeed, *The Godfather* continues to attract new audiences and fresh fans. The epic saga of the Corleone family has become an ingrained part of our cultural lexicon and has been massively influential. The mafia genre, in its modern form, owes its existence to *The Godfather*, with films such as *Once Upon a Time in America* (1984), *Goodfellas* (1990) and, more recently, the hugely popular television series *The Sopranos* (1999–2007) all direct descendants of Coppola's master-piece. A handful of quotes from the trilogy – such as 'Luca Brasi sleeps with the fishes' and 'I'll make him an offer he can't refuse' – have become part of our daily language. The latter remains, quite simply, one of the most memorable film quotes of all time.

Continued interest in the *Godfather* phenomenon is reflected in the strong worldwide market in related memorabilia. Original posters for *The Godfather* are always in high demand, with prices rising steadily. At an auction of Marlon Brando's personal effects held at Christie's, New York in June 2005, there was a real buzz about the section of the auction related to *Godfather* memorabilia, and the bidding went through the roof. The actor's working script realized $265,000 – more than twenty times the estimate of $10,000–15,000, while a belt engraved with the words 'Mighty Moon Champion' – made by Robert Duvall and James Caan and given to Brando as a gift – sold for $2,500, more than ten times the original estimate. (Brando is said to have started a craze for mooning during filming, bearing his behind to over 500 extras during the filming of the wedding scene alone.) A letter from Mario Puzo to Marlon Brando (see opposite), asking him to consider playing the role of Don Vito Corleone, raised $110,000 – more than 100 times the estimate of $800–1,200.

The massive success of the *Godfather* movies launched the careers of several actors – Al Pacino, Robert De Niro, Diane Keaton and Andy Garcia among others – who have gone on to become massive A-list stars. At the same time, the movies embraced a wealth of old Hollywood talent, with established actors such as Marlon Brando, Richard Conte, John Marley and Eli Wallach adding weight and class to the films. Perhaps the main reason *The Godfather* continues to attract such interest today, however, is simply the quality and beauty of the filmmaking; a powerful combination of sharp writing, brilliant performances and a remarkable depth and richness in lighting. Collecting together stills, publicity photographs and artwork – many of which have never been published before – this book aims to capture some of that magic; and to provide some insight into the qualities that draw viewers back to Coppola's masterpiece time and time again.

TONY NOURMAND

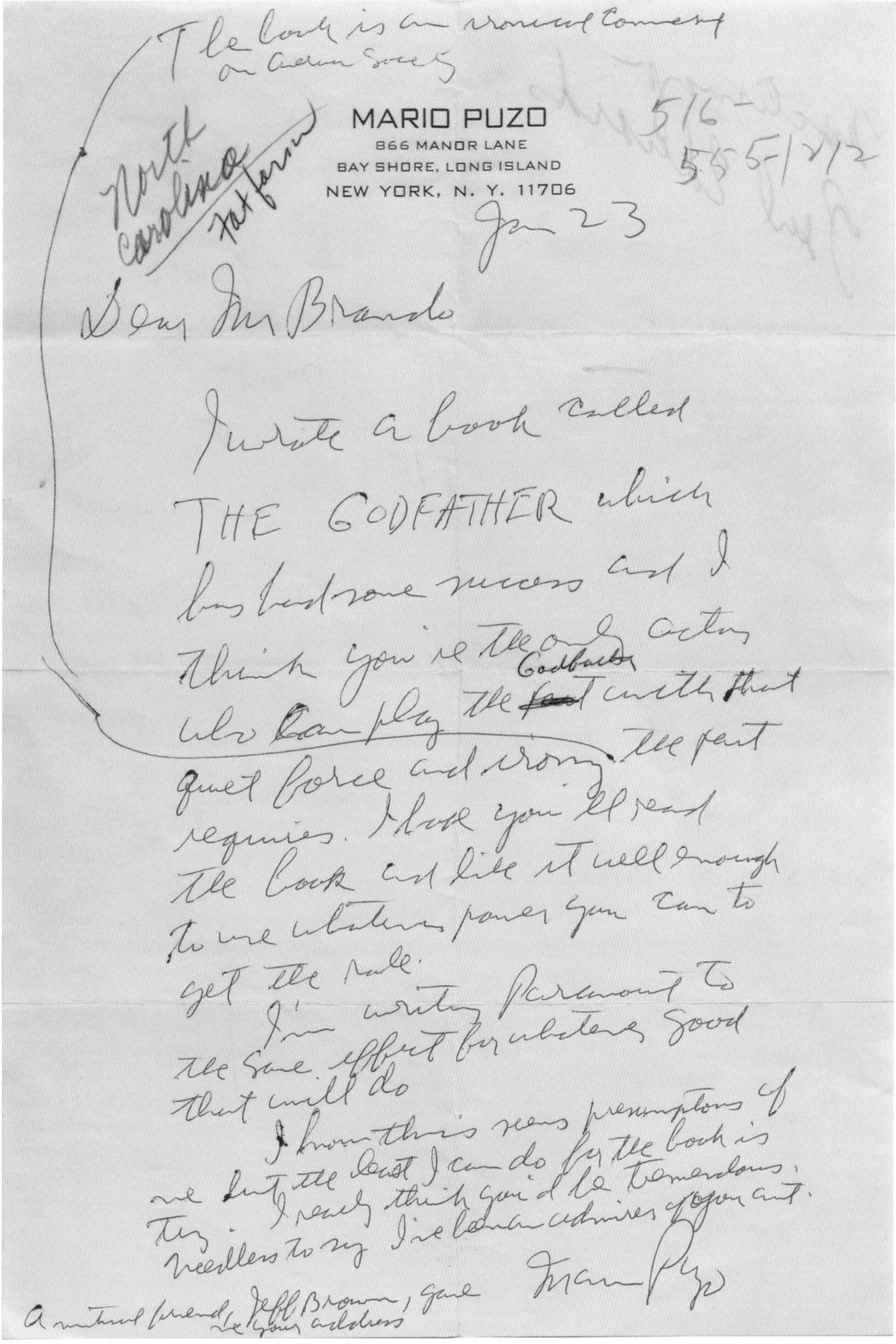

The book is an ironical comment
on American society

North
Carolina
fat farm

MARIO PUZO
866 MANOR LANE
BAY SHORE, LONG ISLAND
NEW YORK, N. Y. 11706

516—
555-1212

Jan 23

Dear Mr Brando

I wrote a book called
THE GODFATHER which
has had some success and I
think you're the only actor
who can play the ~~part~~ Godfather with that
quiet force and irony the part
requires. I hope you'll read
the book and like it well enough
to use whatever power you can to
get the role.
        I'm writing Paramount to
the same effect for whatever good
that will do
        I know this seems presumptuous of
me but the least I can do for the book is
try. I really think you'd be tremendous.
Needless to say I've been an admirer of your art.

        Mario Puzo

A mutual friend, Jeff Brown, gave
me your address

MARIO PUZO, WRITER

Above: Puzo relaxes in front of his typewriter with his trademark cigar, circa 1970.

Opposite: **Time**, 28 August 1978. Cover art by Braldt Bralds. Bralds (b. 1951) moved to the States from his native Holland in 1978, and this **Time** cover was his first commission. He still has a successful and diverse career in illustration today.

Mario Puzo (1920–1999) was born and raised in Hell's Kitchen. Passionate about writing from a young age, Puzo's first published work appeared in *American Vanguard* in 1950. Five years later he published his first book, *Dark Arena*, followed by his second novel, *Fortunate Pilgrim*, in 1964. Both were critically acclaimed, but were not financial successes, leaving Puzo struggling to support his family alongside a crippling gambling habit. His decision to write the much more commercial *The Godfather* was thus as much a financial choice as an artistic one.

The Godfather was based on mafia anecdotes Puzo had accumulated during his time as a pulp journalist and was so vivid, most people refused to believe that Puzo had never been involved in the underworld himself. G.P. Putnam's and Sons publishers loved his ideas and offered him a $5,000 advance on the strength of a ten-page draft outline for the project. Sixty pages into the text, Puzo sold the film rights to Paramount for $12,500 and when the book was completed, Putnam's paid him a record-breaking $410,000 for the paperback rights. *The Godfather* became an overnight sensation and remained on the *New York Times* bestseller list for sixty-seven weeks. Puzo was hired by Paramount to work on the script for the movie version, ultimately winning two Oscars for Best Writing for *The Godfather* and *The Godfather: Part II* (both awards were shared with Coppola).

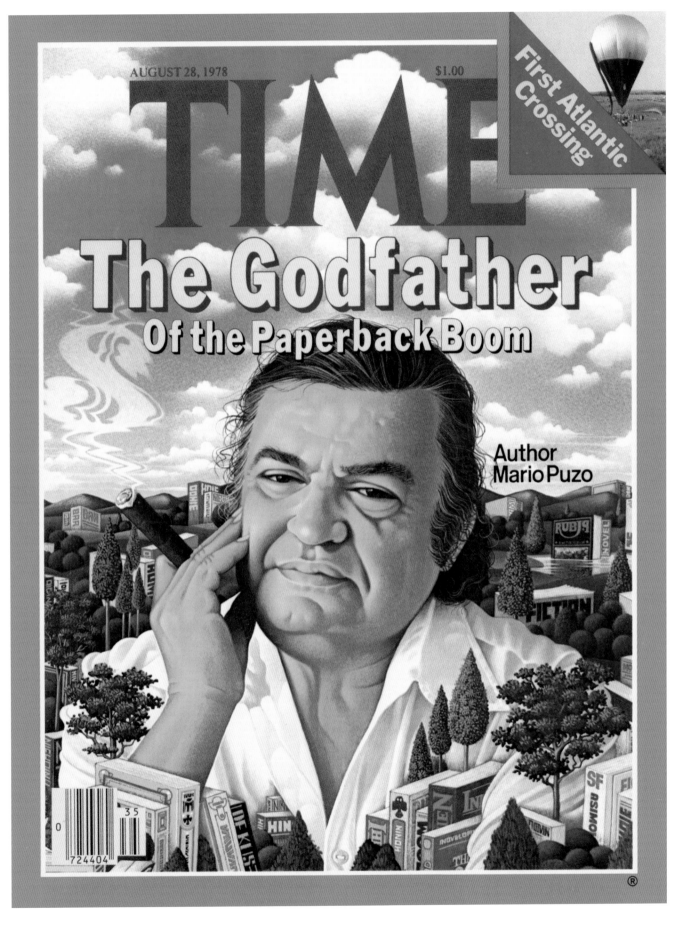

ROBERT EVANS, MOVIE EXECUTIVE

Born in New York, **Robert Evans** (b.1930) began his career as a teenage radio actor. With his classic good looks and winning smile, he first flirted with a movie career in his early twenties. However, after failing to get a break, he turned to modelling and then business, working for his brother's successful clothing company. This turned him into a millionaire before the age of twenty-five. It was while on a business trip in Beverly Hills, overseeing the opening of a new clothing boutique, that actress Norma Shearer spotted Evans talking on the phone by the pool at her hotel. She offered him the part of her late husband Irving Thalberg in *The Man of a Thousand Faces* (1957). The movie was a success and secured him other roles, most notably as the lead in *The Fiend Who Walked the West* (1958). However, Evans saw that the real power and money in movies was to be had in producing, and he was determined to break into this side of the industry. He bought the rights to the Roderick Thorp novel *The Detective* and then when Hollywood became interested in the book, used it as leverage to get his foot in the door. When an article appeared in the *New York Times* on the aspiring producer (still before Evans had actually made any films), it caught the attention of Charles Bludhorn, who was head of the conglomerate Gulf & Western, which owned Paramount Pictures.

Liking Evans's style and keen to inject new blood into the studio, Bludhorn offered him the job as head of production at Paramount Pictures. His appointment in such a prestigious position caused uproar in Hollywood. Not only was he perceived as far too young for such a job; he had never produced a picture. Most predicted that he would not survive a month and that the struggling studio would collapse around his ears. However, his critics had not counted on the determined energy and vision of the young 'boy wonder'. Evans focused on embracing new, fresh projects for Paramount and some of the many films he was responsible for include *The Odd Couple* (1968), *Rosemary's Baby* (1968), *Love Story* (1970), *Harold and Maude* (1971), *The Godfather* (1972) and *Serpico* (1973). Under his tenure, Paramount moved from ninth position in the industry to number one; in just a few years, Evans had reversed Paramount's fortunes and repositioned her as one of Hollywood's major players. When he moved into producing in his own right in 1974, he continued to rake in money for the studio, with hits such as *Chinatown* (1974) and *Marathon Man* (1976).

Evans adhered to the old 'work hard, play hard' maxim. He was a chronic workaholic, spending hours on the phone and in meetings both in the office and at home. Indeed, so frequently did he conduct business from his own estate that his colleagues referred to it as Paramount West. Despite this, Evans also managed to have a colourful private life and he has been connected to countless beautiful women over the years, including Ava Gardner, Lana Turner and Grace Kelly. He has been married seven times, most notably to Ali MacGraw at the height of her fame. (She left him in 1972 for Steve McQueen).

By the eighties, Evans's 'sex, drugs and rock 'n' roll' lifestyle was beginning to escalate out of control, with a cocaine addiction and rumours of involvement in a murder scandal. Ever the dogged fighter, however, he fought his way back from the threat of obscurity and by the nineties had negotiated a new deal with Paramount. This decade also saw the release of his bestselling autobiography, *The Kid Stays in the Picture*, which was turned into an award-winning documentary of the same name in 2002.

Opposite: Robert Evans working by the pool at his Hollywood home.

ALBERT S. RUDDY, PRODUCER

As shooting began on *The Godfather*, Paramount were inundated with letters and petitions from angry Italian-Americans across America, claiming the film belittled all that had been achieved for Italian-American rights. The Italian-American Civil Rights League in New York organized a rally in Madison Square Gardens that raised over $600,000 for the sole purpose of stopping the film. Boycotts, strikes and more demonstrations were threatened and the production was in considerable danger of drawing to a standstill. Producer Al Ruddy was given the task of trying to address the problem.

Ruddy met with Anthony Colombo of the Italian-American Civil Rights League. Anthony was the son of Joseph Colombo Sr – founder of the League, community- and business leader, advocate for Italian-American rights and, reputedly, head of one of the real mafia families in New York. In his meetings with Tony Colombo, Ruddy agreed to remove all references to 'mafia' or 'Cosa Nostra' from the film. He also granted the League access to the script and agreed that the proceeds of the New York premiere would be donated to the League's hospital fund.

When news of the deal broke, the press had a field day, accusing Ruddy of negotiating with the mafia. The studio was livid and he very nearly paid for the scandal with his job. Ruddy had, though, effectively guaranteed that filming could now continue uninterrupted and all protests, action and the threat of action vanished overnight.

Born in Montreal in 1930 and raised in New York, producer **Albert S. Ruddy**'s career trajectory was not naturally headed towards Hollywood. With a background in chemical engineering and construction, Ruddy only entered the entertainment industry after a chance meeting with Jack Warner landed him a job as an executive at Warner Brothers. His next break came when Marlon Brando Sr (the actor's father and a film executive) approached him to produce *Wild Seed* (1965). Ruddy then created the television series *Hogan's Heroes*, which proved a massive hit and ran for over five years.

By the time Ruddy was asked to work on *The Godfather*, he had produced two more successful low-budget films, *Little Fauss and Big Halsy* (1970) and *Making It* (1971). Although still relatively inexperienced, Ruddy had established an excellent reputation for being innovative and able to work within a tight budget, qualities that would stand him in good stead for *The Godfather*. The studio also saw him as a suitable counterbalance to Coppola, reining in the director's more expensive and grandiose ideas.

The success of *The Godfather* secured Ruddy a Best Picture Oscar. He has since gone on to work on several hit films and television series, including *The Longest Yard* (1974), *The Cannonball Run* (1981), *Walker, Texas Ranger* (1993–2001) and more recently the critically acclaimed *Million Dollar Baby* (2004), for which he was again given the Academy Award for Best Picture.

Above: Producer Al Ruddy on set in discussion with Brando and Coppola.

Opposite: Ruddy relaxing in his office, circa 1971.

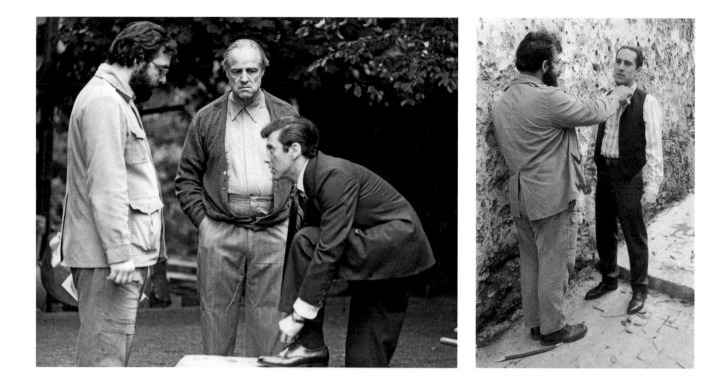

FRANCIS FORD COPPOLA, DIRECTOR

The legendary **Francis Ford Coppola** (b.1939) was a key player in the 'New Hollywood' that evolved in the late sixties and early seventies. This movement injected the industry with a fresh energy and realism and sought to incorporate the artistic freedom and spirit of independent filmmaking into the bigger Hollywood studio system.

Raised in an artistic family, Francis was a keen playwright from childhood. Offered a scholarship to Hofstra University on the strength of plays he had written at school, he graduated in 1959 with a BA in Theatre Arts. Allegedly inspired to become a director after watching Eisenstein's Russian epic *Oktober*, he began an MA at UCLA Film School at the age of twenty-one. His big break came two years later when producer Roger Corman contacted the film department looking for someone to subtitle a Russian film he had recently purchased for the American market, *Nebo Zovyot*. Coppola was chosen for the job and, having no knowledge of Russian, wrote a completely fresh script. Corman was so impressed, he credited him as associate producer on the film, which was released as *Battle Beyond the Sun* (1960). After working on a number of 'nudie-cuties' with Corman, Coppola's first directorial credit was with the B-hit *Dementia 13* (1963). In 1966, he wrote and directed his first 'proper' work, *You're a Big Boy Now*. Although something of a commercial failure, the film was critically acclaimed and well received at Cannes.

The director was rapidly earning a reputation as an emerging talent. In 1969, Warner Brothers gave Coppola money to set up American Zoetrope with fellow movie brat George Lucas. However, after Coppola's *The Rain People* (1969) and Lucas's *THX-1138* (1971) made little impact at the box office, and after previewing the scripts for *Apocalypse Now* and *The Conversation*, Warner demanded their money back.

Massively in debt, when *The Godfather* project came along it was the perfect opportunity for Coppola and, despite his initial reluctance, proved a huge success. The film was a critical triumph, with Coppola lauded as a genius and nominated for an Academy Award for Best Director. It was also a commercial success and with a six per cent share in the profits, Coppola's fortunes literally changed overnight. He had definitively proved that auteur filmmaking and money-making blockbusters could go hand in hand.

Above Left: Coppola with Marlon Brando and Al Pacino on set.
Above Right: Coppola stands in an alley and holds a knife to Robert De Niro's throat to illustrate how to kill a man properly while directing him on location in Sicily.

Opposite: Coppola takes a break from filming the assassination of Sonny Corleone.

THE MAKING OF THE GODFATHER

In the mid-sixties, Hollywood was suffering something of a crisis in confidence. Turn-over was low, unemployment high and the industry was stagnating. Keen to reverse their flagging fortunes, Paramount's response was to seek out new and innovative projects. When approached with a draft of a new book by the critically acclaimed but little-known author Mario Puzo, it seemed the perfect venture they were looking for.

Puzo's new book, *The Godfather*, was a powerful and violent tale about the mafia. However, Paramount's initial enthusiasm for the project vanished after the disastrous box-office failure of *The Brotherhood* in 1968, a gangster flick with a nominally similar plot-line. The project was shelved. Then, when Puzo's book hit the shelves in 1969 and became an overnight sensation, Paramount once again sat down to re-evaluate their options.

Deciding to go ahead with the project, Paramount were nonetheless still cautious over the poor performance of *The Brotherhood* and insisted that *The Godfather* was low budget (under $1 million), set in the present and filmed on the studio backlot. Next they had to find a director and the studio exhausted almost all of their options before finally turning to Francis Ford Coppola. Those considered included Lewis Gilbert (*You Only Live Twice*, 1967), Constantin Costa-Gavras (*Z*, 1969), Fred Zinnemann (*A Man For All Seasons*, 1966), Peter Yates (*Bullitt*, 1968), Arthur Penn (*Bonnie and Clyde*, 1967), Richard Brooks (*In Cold Blood*, 1967) and Elia Kazan (*The Arrangement*, 1969). Many of those approached refused, nervous of adapting such a well-loved book. Puzo's glorification of violence was also seen as a decidedly risky factor.

Coppola had a reputation for rapidly absorbing studio budgets with his grand ideas, but Paramount were finally won over by the fact that he himself was relatively affordable (Coppola desperately needed the work to repay his Zoetrope debts to Warner), he was Italian-American and instinctively knew the subject matter, and he had an indisputable talent as a writer, so could work with Puzo on developing the script.

With Coppola on board, the project took on a new and inevitable momentum. The budget was soon pushed to over $6 million, Coppola convinced Paramount that the film could only work as a period piece and within weeks, cast and crew were heading east to shoot on location in the streets of New York.

Opposite: Clemenza kisses Michael's hand after he is declared head of the Corleone family.

THE GODFATHER SAGA

Above: A young Vito Corleone at the funeral procession of his father, murdered for an insult to the local mafia chief Don Francesco Ciccio.

Opposite: The funeral march is interrupted when Vito's older brother is slaughtered for attempting to avenge his father's death. Vito and his mother flee the scene.

The *Godfather* saga is centred on the twin themes of family and power. It tells the story of Vito Corleone, forced to flee Sicily for America as a young boy. The 'Land of Opportunity' opens its doors to Vito's entrepreneurial spirit and over the next twenty years, he builds a vast empire of underworld contacts and businesses, eventually becoming the head of one of the most powerful mafia families on the East Coast. Despite such dubious foundations, Vito represents a noble kind of morality that has love for one's family at its very heart. He conducts his business within a moral framework and although his actions involve murder and criminality, they still appear honourable.

In his dotage, Vito hands power to his eldest son Michael, who takes over the family empire. Through Michael's tenure as Godfather, the mafia's ugly underbelly is properly exposed and his story becomes one of moral and personal decay. His actions and those of the world he inhabits are revealed as truly repugnant and he becomes increasingly isolated in his damnation. As he ages, Michael tries to seek a level of redemption. Ultimately, however, the magnitude of his sins destroys him and he dies shattered and alone.

Taken together as a trilogy, *The Godfather* is often viewed as something of a morality tale that symbolizes the history of America itself. Vito reigns over the Corleone family at a time in America's past that is noble and just; through her intervention in the Second World War, America is seen as the saviour of the world, representing all that is good and pure. By the time Michael begins his rise to power in the late 1950s, America has entered the ethical quagmire of the Cold War and is taking its first tentative steps into the political minefield that is Vietnam. Michael's damnation, therefore, can be seen as a reflection of the loss of America's own moral compass.

ROBERT DE NIRO, ACTOR

Robert De Niro had auditioned for the first *Godfather* movie and had been a strong contender for the role of Sonny. He was eventually cast in a smaller role but asked to be released when he landed the lead in another film. This proved fortunate as it ultimately left De Niro free to play the young Vito Corleone in *The Godfather: Part II*, a part for which he was honoured with an Academy Award for Best Supporting Actor.

Born in New York, **Robert De Niro** (b.1943) was encouraged to express himself from a young age by his artistic parents. He developed an interest in acting and the movies after being taken to the cinema regularly as a child and at thirteen his mother enrolled him at New York's prestigious High School of Music and Art. However, not yet mature enough for the rigour of serious study, De Niro dropped out and hung around with a local street gang (where he was known by the moniker 'Bobby Milk' for his pale complexion). Despite his troubled school life, his passion for acting continued to develop during this period and at sixteen he landed his first paid acting job in a tour of Chekhov's *The Bear*.

Attending the Stella Adler Conservatory, De Niro became a devoted follower of method acting, a trademark of his work throughout his career. His talent attracted the attention of Brian de Palma, who cast him, aged twenty, in *The Wedding Party*. Although filmed in 1963, the movie was not actually released until six years later, making De Niro's official screen debut de Palma's *Greetings* (1968).

After his three collaborations with De Palma (he also starred in the director's *Hi, Mom!* [1969]), De Niro's next significant break came after landing the lead as a dying baseball player in *Bang the Drum Slowly* (1973). Such was the power and impact of his performance that Martin Scorsese approached the actor to star in his new film *Mean Streets* (1973). Thus began one of the greatest partnerships in cinema with their fruitful collaboration producing such compelling classics as *Taxi Driver* (1976), *Raging Bull* (1980) and *Goodfellas* (1990).

De Niro displays a relentless dedication to understanding the characters he plays; to research the role of Vito Corleone, he moved to a small town in Sicily; for the role of Jake La Motta in *Raging Bull* he gained sixty pounds and for *New York, New York* (1977) he learned to play the saxophone. It is this dedication, combined with a remarkable talent, that has made him such a powerhouse star, and has seen him win two Best Actor Academy Awards and garner a further four nominations. He is regarded as one of the greatest and most gifted actors of his generation. In addition to *The Godfather: Part II* and his work with Scorsese, other mesmeric performances include *The Deer Hunter* (1978), *Once Upon a Time in America* (1984), *Cape Fear* (1991) as well as comic turns in *Midnight Run* (1988) and *Meet the Parents* (2000).

Above Left: Vito prepares to assassinate the local Black Hand boss, Fanucci. Above Middle: Vito with his family in Sicily. Above Right: Vito working at a local grocers in New York's Little Italy, circa 1917.

Opposite: Don Vito presents himself to Don Ciccio, before avenging his father's death.

Above: Fanucci strolls through Little Italy, which he rules by terrorizing local businesses and families.

Opposite: Gastone Moschin as Fanucci.

For authenticity, Coppola wanted to cast an Italian actor in the role of Fanucci, and chose the talented **Gastone Moschin** (b.1929). Born in Verona, Moschin studied at the Academy of Dramatic Arts in Rome. He has had a successful and diverse career in theatre, film and television, winning several awards including two Nastri D'Argento Awards for Best Supporting Actor. His best-known films internationally include *The Godfather: Part II* and Bernardo Bertolucci's *The Conformist* (1970). He continues to remain in demand today, and also teaches Cinema Studies at the MUMOS acting school he co-founded in Terni, central Italy.

THE MAKING OF THE GODFATHER: PART II

Above: Fanucci is murdered by Vito while the neighbourhood is distracted by a street party.

Opposite: Vito getting ready to fire the fatal bullet.

The Godfather's phenomenal success finally earned Coppola Paramount's trust and *The Godfather: Part II* was free of many of the arguments and interfering that had plagued the filming of the first movie. On *Part II*, Coppola was given more money and greater artistic freedom, allowing him to explore the ambitious concept of incorporating two distinct storylines (Vito's and Michael's) into one film.

Due to exhibitors's advances, *The Godfather: Part II* was in profit even before it was released. Expectations were high, and the movie did not disappoint. It opened to rave reviews, with many claiming it was even better than the first film, an unheard-of feat for a sequel. The film won six Academy Awards, including Best Picture and Best Director, and received a further five nominations.

Above & Opposite: Vito sports a moustache as a symbol of his new Don status. The neighbourhood businessmen respect his authority by refusing money for goods and services.

Much has been made of the symbolic role that oranges play in *The Godfather* trilogy and theories abound that the fruit are always shown in a significant scene. For example, when Vito is gunned down in *The Godfather* he has been buying oranges from a local grocer, while in *The Godfather: Part II*, he is handed an orange by a fruit-seller to symbolize his new Don status. In *The Godfather: Part III*, an orange rolls from Michael's hand in his death scene. Despite such academic speculation, however, production designer Dean Tavoularis explained it much more simply by claiming it was a technical device to add some much-needed colour and contrast to otherwise dark scenes.

Above: Vito kisses the hand of Don Ciccio, before stabbing him to death.

Opposite: Vito takes his family to his birth place, the town of Corleone in Sicily.

THE CASTING OF VITO CORLEONE

As excitement over *The Godfather* project grew, so too did interest in the lead role of Don Vito Corleone, and every middle-aged actor in the business wanted a shot at it. Those that were seriously considered include Laurence Olivier (who was ill at the time), John Marley and Richard Conte (who both ultimately landed smaller parts in the film). Coppola, however, envisaged just one man in the role; he believed Marlon Brando alone was capable of bringing the necessary gravitas and depth to the performance.

Brando had a reputation for being extremely difficult to work with, notoriously causing productions to over run by being late, disagreeable and causing conflict. He was also expensive, and after a series of bad career choices in the sixties (including such disasters as *The Appaloosa* [1966] and *The Night of the Following Day* [1968]), the studio was not even convinced that he was worth paying for. When Coppola refused to back down, Paramount finally relented by stipulating three conditions: Brando would not receive a large salary, but rather a percentage of the gross; he would be financially responsible for any production delays he caused; and he would have to take a screen test. This final stipulation was their trump card, as Brando famously refused to test for roles in such a way. However, when Coppola turned up at Brando's house with a hand-held camera and asked him to interpret the character, Brando put some shoe polish in his hair and tissues in his cheeks and instantly turned into the Don in his own living room. The transformation was astonishing and when the studio saw the footage, they were blown away, finally agreeing that Brando was the only actor capable of doing proper justice to the role.

Above: The actors considered for the role of Vito Corleone. Clockwise from top left: John Marley, Richard Conte, Anthony Quinn, Ernest Borgnine, Raf Vallone, George C. Scott, Sir Laurence Olivier, Carlo Ponti. All photographs circa 1970.

Opposite: Marlon Brando circa 1970.

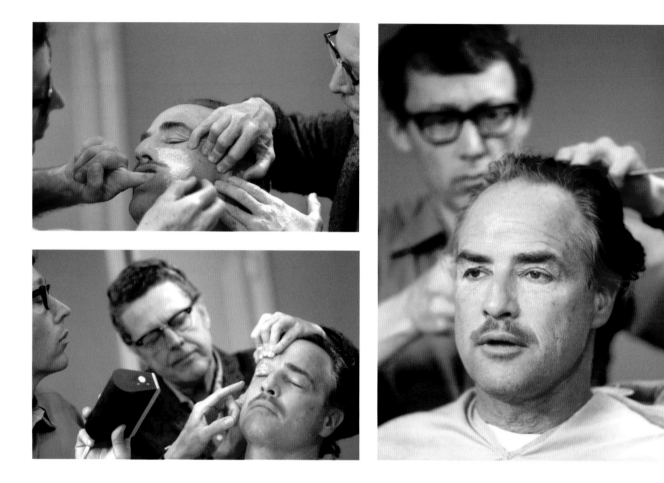

DICK SMITH, MAKE-UP ARTIST

The Oscar-winning **Dick Smith** (b.1922) is one of the most influential make-up artists in television and cinema history. He is a pioneer in new techniques, particularly in the use of latex and plastic, and has worked hard to open up the trade to newcomers, running professional make-up courses, publishing books on the art of make-up and nurturing the talent of such protégés as Rick Baker. Smith has been nominated for several Oscars for his work on such diverse films as *The Godfather* (1972), *The Exorcist* (1973), *Taxi Driver* (1976), *The Deer Hunter* (1978), *Amadeus* (1984) and *The Cotton Club* (1984).

It was while studying pre-medicine at Yale (with a view to becoming a dentist), that Smith found a book on the movie make-up of the classic Universal monsters of the thirties and became hooked. He began working for the university theatre group and at weekends would practise on himself, making-up as one of the old monsters and heading out into the street to gauge people's reactions.

Smith at first struggled to break into the profession, as its secrets were jealously guarded by those already in the trade. However, this only challenged him to develop his own innovative techniques and by 1945 he had been appointed make-up director for NBC, a role he held for fourteen years. His most famous assignment during this time was making-up President Franklin D. Roosevelt during the 1948 Democratic National Convention.

Smith's particular speciality is ageing. For *Little Big Man* (1970) he turned Dustin Hoffman from a sprightly thirty into a crumbling 121-year-old. For his work on *The Godfather*, he spent over an hour and a half with Brando each morning, ageing the actor's face with layers of liquid latex and a dental device called a 'plumber' to make his jowls droop. Such was the transformation Smith created, that Brando was able to eat in the local restaurants around set without being recognised.

Above & opposite: Make-up artist Dick Smith ageing Brando for the role of Vito.

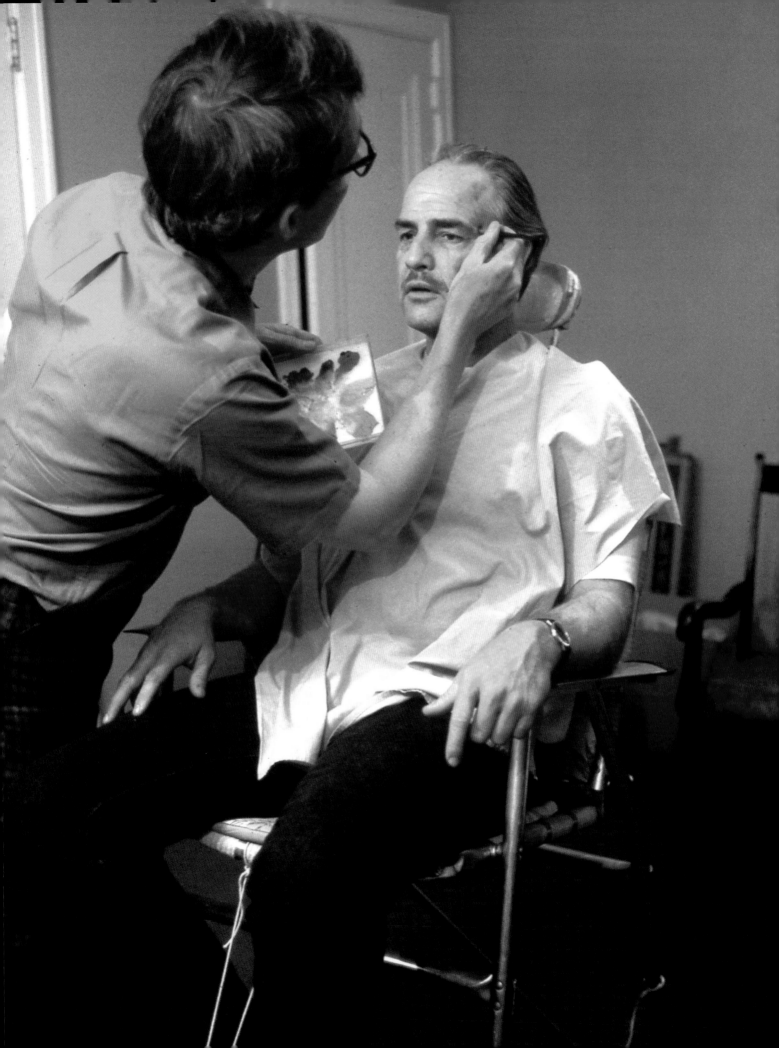

MARLON BRANDO, ACTOR

Marlon Brando (1924–2004) is perhaps the greatest film actor of all time. He revolutionized the film actors' landscape and his methods set a new benchmark in quality and talent to which successive generations of young actors still aspire.

Frequently in trouble as a boy, Brando was expelled from military academy in his teens, and eventually moved to New York to follow his aspirations of becoming an actor. He studied at the Actors Studio and New School Dramatic Workshop under Stella Adler, where he learned the method techniques that would make his acting style so renowned. His theatre work was critically acclaimed: lauded as Broadway's most promising actor, his most impressive and rousing stage performance was in 1947 as Stanley Kowalski in *A Streetcar Named Desire*.

Three years later, Brando made his screen debut as a crippled veteran in *The Men*. As research for the role, he spent a month in bed at a veteran's hospital. This powerful performance set the standard for his work over the next decade and as the fifties progressed, so too did his reputation. He was nominated for an Academy Award for Best Actor four years running: for Elia Kazan's film version of *A Streetcar Named Desire* (1951), then for *Viva Zapata!* (1952), *Julius Caesar* (1953) and *On the Waterfront* (1954). *On the Waterfront* saw him finally win the award and is still regarded as one of the greatest performances ever recorded on celluloid. The 1950s also saw Brando in one of his most influential roles as Johnny Strabler in *The Wild One* (1953). The original rebel without a cause, Brando's specific take on disaffected youth influenced a whole generation, with supposedly even Elvis and James Dean idolizing him.

The sixties were less kind to Brando. He failed repeatedly at the box office and his critics increasingly accused him of squandering his enormous talent. It was at this relative low-point in his career that Coppola snapped him up for the role of Don Corleone in *The Godfather*. Brando's performance won him the Oscar for Best Actor and saw a brief resurgence in his career, including the critically acclaimed, but controversial *Last Tango In Paris*, released the following year.

Around this time, however, Brando turned his back on the industry, retreating into the reclusiveness that was to mark his later years. His life became increasingly characterised by eccentricities, family crises and obesity and from the mid-seventies onwards, Brando returned to Hollywood on only a few occasions, most notably for *Superman* (1978) and *Apocalypse Now* (1979). For his small part in *Superman*, Brando set a new salary record, securing a staggering $3.7 million, plus 16.86% of the gross. When the film proved a huge success, it meant Brando effectively earned $14 million for twelve days' work. The fact that he could demand such sums is testament to the force of Brando's talent, and his lasting legacy is as one of Hollywood's greatest-ever screen actors.

Above left: Bonasera kisses Vito's hand after asking for his help during Connie Corleone's wedding. Above middle: Vito plays with his grandson Anthony in the garden, shortly before his death. Above right: Bonasera pleads with Vito.

Opposite: Vito conducts business from his office at the Genko headquarters.

THE CASTING OF MICHAEL CORLEONE

Above: The actors considered for the role of Michael Corleone. Top, left to right: Alain Delon, Jack Nicholson, Warren Beatty. Middle, left to right: Martin Sheen, Robert Redford, Ryan O'Neal. Bottom, left to right: Dustin Hoffman, Dean Stockwell, David Carradine. All photographs circa 1970.

*Opposite: Al Pacino on set during filming of the first **Godfather**.*

No sooner had Coppola won his stand-off with Paramount over the casting of Brando, than he began a new round of arguments over who should play Michael. Several actors were considered for the role, including Robert Redford, Warren Beatty, Jack Nicholson, Robert De Niro and Dustin Hoffman. However, Coppola believed the dark, brooding quality of the character could only be properly conveyed by a little-known Italian-American actor, Al Pacino.

Although developing a reputation as a respected theatre actor, Pacino had only appeared in one feature film to that date, *The Panic In Needle Park* (1971), in which he played a homeless junkie. Coppola saw in Pacino a talent and quality that he believed would be perfect for Michael. However, when the young actor was given a screen test, he was allegedly under-prepared and fluffed his lines. The studio were convinced he was totally wrong for the part: too short, too ugly, too Italian-American and a bad actor. Coppola famously called him a 'self-destructive bastard', but was still convinced he was right for the role. After screen-testing repeatedly, and repeatedly failing to convey any sense of his inherent talent, Pacino only secured the role after Coppola forced everyone at Paramount to sit through *The Panic In Needle Park*.

Even after Pacino was safely on set, he was followed around by sniggering and vicious comments from cast and crew. It was only when Michael comes into his own as the Don's heir apparent, that Pacino's power and genius as an actor was given room to shine and his critics were thoroughly silenced.

THE CASTING OF KAY ADAMS

Above: The actresses considered for the role of Kay Adams. Clockwise from top left: Ali MacGraw, Cybill Shepherd, Geneviève Bujold, Karen Black, Jill Clayburgh and Michelle Phillips. All photographs circa 1970.

Opposite: Diane Keaton circa 1970.

Several actresses were considered for the role of Kay Adams. Jill Clayburgh was a strong contender (she was also dating Pacino at the time), as was Ali MacGraw (fresh from her success in *Love Story*). Diane Keaton was a favourite from the start, except with cinematographer Gordon Willis, who claimed she was gawky and that he would have to shoot her from the waist upwards. However, Coppola saw in Diane Keaton the quirky, intelligent *Annie Hall* qualities that he believed the character should embody. She went on to star as Kay in all three *Godfather* films.

Above: The Corleone family line up at the wedding of Connie Corleone for one of the most famous wedding photographs in history.

Opposite: **Mad** *Magazine, #155, December 1972. Cover art by Norman Mingo.*

A veteran of World War I, **Norman Mingo** (1896–1980) had a diverse career as an artist, illustrating pin-ups, book-jackets and covers for publications such as *American Weekly* and *Ladies Home Journal* and working for various advertising agencies. He remains most famous for creating the much-loved *Mad* magazine mascot Alfred E. Neuman in 1956. Mingo left the magazine a year later, but returned in 1962 and designed the majority of *Mad*'s covers until 1976.

The magazine has always been famous for its movie tie-in covers, that pay tribute to the biggest film releases of the day by incorporating Alfred E. Neuman into a key scene. For *The Godfather* cover, he stars as a child at the wedding of Connie Corleone.

No. 155 Dec. '72 33230

MAD

OUR PRICE 40¢ CHEAP

IN THIS ISSUE WE BLAST... The Godfather

TALIA SHIRE, ACTRESS

Top left: Connie Corleone defends herself against her abusive first husband Carlo Rizzi. Top right: Connie in her later years. Bottom left: Connie at a party to celebrate her nephew Anthony's first Communion. Bottom right: Connie supports her illegitimate nephew Vincent Mancini as he is introduced to Michael.

Opposite: Connie and Carlo pose for a wedding photograph.

Connie Corleone was played by Coppola's own sister **Talia Shire** (b.1946, she takes her surname from her first marriage to the composer David Shire). The youngest in the family, Shire originally had dreams of becoming a choreographer before being offered a scholarship to the Yale School of Drama. Although she developed a genuine love of acting, she found the course stifling and dropped out in her second year to move to Hollywood. Just as her brother had been given his start in Hollywood by Roger Corman, so too did Shire start out playing bit parts in a number of the director's B-movies.

Shire landed the role of Connie in *The Godfather* after asking her brother for a screen test. Although initially reluctant, believing her too beautiful for the role, he was easily won over by her obvious talent and she was given the part. Shire starred in all three *Godfather* films and the vulnerability and honesty she brought to the role secured her an Academy Award nomination for Best Supporting Actress in *The Godfather: Part II*. She is also renowned for playing Adrian Balboa in the *Rocky* movies, a role for which she was again nominated for an Academy Award.

SINATRA AND THE GODFATHER

Above: Frank Sinatra takes a stroll along the Miami beachfront during a break from filming **The Lady in Cement** (1968). The singer is with his minders and his stand-in, who is wearing an identical outfit to him.

Opposite: Al Martino as Johnny Fontaine. Martino shot to fame in 1952 with the first number one single in the first ever UK singles chart. Still a popular singer around the world today, Martino's best-known hits have included **Spanish Eyes** and **Volare**.

The character of Johnny Fontaine was allegedly based on Frank Sinatra. Monitored closely by the FBI throughout his career, Sinatra was famously close friends with several key mob figures and the depth of his involvement is still hotly debated to this day. It was also suggested at the time (perhaps unfairly, considering his talent) that Sinatra had landed the role of Maggio in *From Here To Eternity* (1953) by employing the help of mafia buddy Frank Costello (just as Don Corleone helps Fontaine).

Before the release of *The Godfather*, Sinatra had his office write a letter to Puzo's publishers demanding to see a copy of the text. The publisher refused and Puzo thought little more of it. A few months later, he found himself at a party where Sinatra was also a guest. The millionaire host was keen to introduce Puzo to the singer and refused to take no for an answer. Puzo himself recounted the ensuing conversation in an article for *New York* magazine in August 1972:

Millionaire: I'd like you to meet my good friend, Mario Puzo.

Sinatra (not looking up): I don't think so.

Millionaire (misunderstanding): I'd like you to meet...

Sinatra: I don't want to meet him.

Millionaire (now in tears): Frank, I'm sorry. God Frank, I didn't know, Frank, I'm sorry...'

Sinatra: It's not your fault.

Puzo: Listen, it wasn't my idea.

Sinatra (misunderstanding): Who told you to put that in the book, your publisher?

Sinatra at this point lost control and started yelling at Puzo until the writer left the party.

Despite the vehemence of his reaction to the book's insinuations, Sinatra remained a fan of *The Godfather* movie, and at one point had even wanted to buy the rights and make the film himself. Another time, he is alleged to have told Coppola that if asked, he would play the Don for him. Much later, he was also seriously considered for the role of Don Altobello in *The Godfather: Part III*.

JOHN MARLEY, ACTOR

Above: Coppola talks John Marley through the bedroom scene, while a fake horse's head rests on the bed.

Opposite: Marley, as Jack Woltz, wakes up to discover the head of his prize racehorse Khartoum resting at the end of his bed.

John Marley (1907–1984) came to *The Godfather* as a respected character actor. Indeed, along with fellow cast member Richard Conte, he had been a contender for the role of Don Corleone himself. Born and raised in Harlem, Marley had worked as a small-time actor in a number of films before he hit the big time in the 1960s (when he was already into his fifties). In 1968, he won Best Actor at the Venice Film Festival for his role in John Cassavetes's breakthrough work *Faces*. Two years later, he was Oscar-nominated for his role in *Love Story* and a year later, he was cast in *The Godfather*. By the end of his career fourteen years later, Marley had starred in over 150 films and television shows.

Marley's key moment in *The Godfather* remains one the most famous scenes in movie history. After refusing to cast Johnny Fontaine in his movie, his character Jack Woltz wakes up to find the head of his prize racehorse Khartoum in bed with him. During rehearsals for the scene a fake head was used, but for the actual day of filming, a real head was borrowed from a local slaughterhouse and the gore was further enhanced with gallons of fake blood.

*Above: Sollozzo approaches
the Corleone family to ask for their
help in building a narcotics empire.*

*Opposite: Al Lettieri as 'The
Turk' Sollozzo.*

Al Lettieri (1928–1975) was the quintessential movie gangster. Allegedly friends with real-life mobsters such as Joey Gallo, the Italian-American Lettieri is most famous for playing villains in *The Getaway* (1972), *Mr Majestyk* (1974), *McQ* (1974) and, of course, as Virgil 'The Turk' Sollozzo in *The Godfather*.

Lettieri was a respected playwright, theatre director and actor for years before making his screen debut aged thirty-six on television's *The Hanged Man*. *The Godfather* proved his big break, but sadly Lettieri was barely getting into his stride as a screen actor when he died of a heart attack aged forty-seven.

JAMES CAAN, ACTOR

Born in the Bronx, **James Caan** (b.1940) was an exceptional sportsman as a teenager and played American football at Michigan University. It was while studying at Hofstra University, however, that he realized his true passion was acting and joined the cast of the Neighborhood Playhouse in New York. Caan began his career in television, before making his silver-screen debut as a bit part in *Irma La Douce* (1963). This was followed by more significant roles in *El Dorado* (1966), Coppola's *The Rain People* (1969) and as the lead in the critically acclaimed television movie *Brian's Song* in 1971 (it was later given a theatrical release).

Caan was one of the key actors Paramount considered for the role of Michael in *The Godfather* and one of the few that Coppola even began to entertain. Although he ultimately cast Pacino in the lead role, Coppola did not want to lose the talented Caan and he was given the part of Sonny – a role for which he was nominated for an Academy Award for Best Supporting Actor. During filming, Caan is said to have spent time with the real-life mobsters who hung around on set, incorporating several of their quirks and mannerisms into his performance. Indeed, it is rumoured that he became such close friends with some mafia types that the FBI had him listed as just another young hood to keep an eye on.

After the success of *The Godfather*, Caan starred in a number of acclaimed movies over the next decade, including *The Gambler* (1974), *Rollerball* (1975), *The Killer Elite* (1975) and Michael Mann's *Thief* (1981). Although taking a break from Hollywood for much of the eighties, he returned to acting in 1988 with *Alien Nation* and his work since then has included *Dick Tracy* (1990), *Misery* (1990), *Bottle Rocket* (1996) and more recently *Dogville* (2003) and *Elf* (2003).

Top left: Sonny Corleone beats up Carlo Rizzi for abusing his sister. This scene left actor Gianni Russo with two cracked ribs and a chipped elbow. Top right: Sonny is gunned down. Bottom left: Coppola directing Caan on the set of **The Godfather: Part II**. Bottom right: Sonny commits adultery with Lucy Mancini, played by actress Jeannie Linero.

Opposite: James Caan on set, doing impressions of James Cagney.

Above: Lenny Montana relaxing on set.

Opposite: Luca Brasi is murdered by Sollozzo's and Tattaglia's men.

Lenny Montana (1926–1992) had no acting experience prior to *The Godfather*. The 6'6" Italian-American professional wrestler was allegedly a genuine mob bodyguard and was cast as Luca Brasi from the scores of gangster extras who milled around set. Montana excelled in the role and went on to star in a further sixteen films.

Montana was petrified of acting with the legendary Brando and in the opening wedding sequence, repeatedly bungled his lines during rehearsal. Coppola shot footage of him practising the scene over and over and then incorporated this into the script so that Montana's stumbling looks like nerves at having to speak to the Don, rather than Brando.

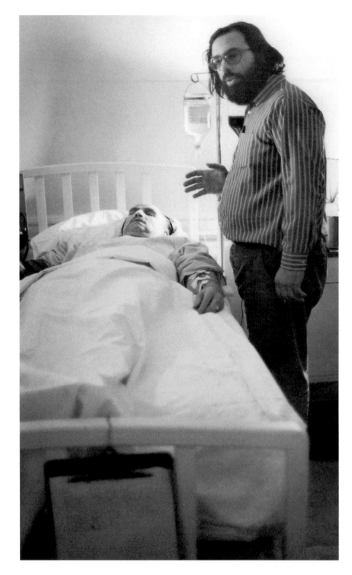

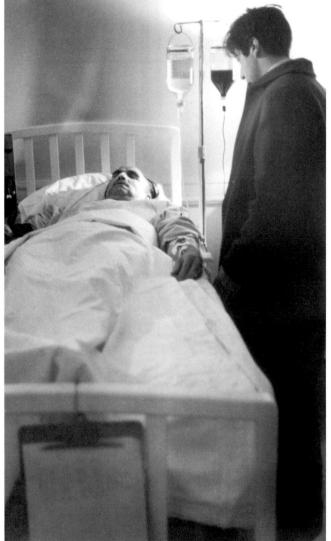

Above left: Coppola directs Pacino as Brando lies motionless in bed. Filmed on location at the Eye and Ear Hospital in New York. Above right: Michael at Vito's bedside after the assassination attempt.

Opposite: Morgana King as Mama Corleone, tending to her husband in his convalescence.

The daughter of a folk musician, **Morgana King** (b.1930) is a jazz singer and actress. Classically trained at the Metropolitan School of Music, she began singing jazz in New York nightclubs in her twenties. Working for almost twenty years as a successful singer, she moved to California in the late 1960s to branch out into acting. She has recorded over thirty albums of jazz music and remains best known for her role as Mama Corleone in *The Godfather* and *The Godfather: Part II*.

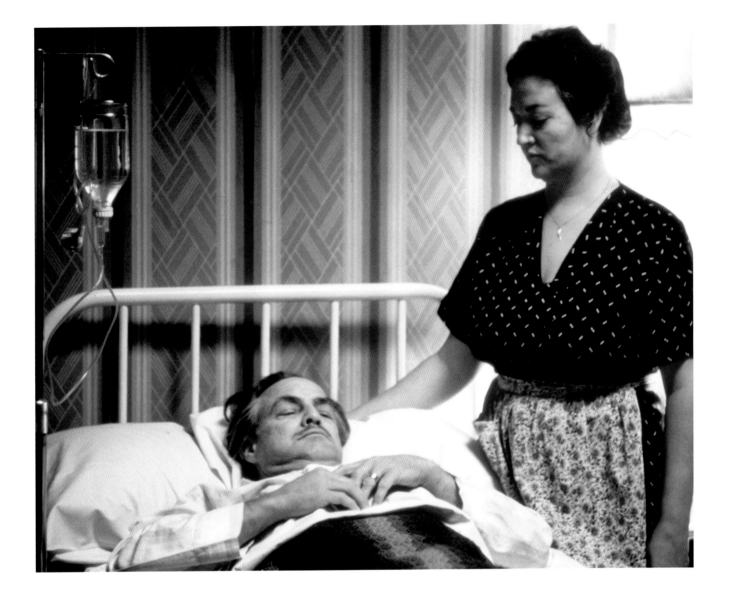

RICHARD S. CASTELLANO & ABE VIGODA, ACTORS

Richard S. Castellano (1933–1988) spent most of his career on the stage and was a respected theatre actor. He worked on only a handful of films during his career and is best remembered for playing Clemenza in *The Godfather* and for uttering the immortal line: "Leave the gun, take the cannoli."

Born in the Bronx, the Italian-American Castellano began his working life as a construction company manager before becoming involved with the New Yiddish Theatre and developing an increasing interest in the stage. In 1969, he won a Tony Award for his performance in *Lovers and Other Strangers* and in 1970, was nominated for an Academy Award for Best Supporting Actor for the film version of the same play.

Clemenza was written out of the script for *The Godfather: Part II* after Castellano is said to have demanded both too high a salary, and that his girlfriend have control over scripting his lines.

Abe Vigoda (b.1921) is best known for playing gangsters and comedic characters. A struggling theatre actor for years, he was given his break in *The Godfather* when he was cast in the part of Sal Tessio from an open audition of over 500 unknowns. After *The Godfather*'s success, he went on to star in his most famous role, that of Fish in the popular American TV series *Barney Miller*.

Above: Richard Castellano as Tessio with a box of the famous cannoli.

Opposite: Abe Vigoda relaxes on set.

STERLING HAYDEN, ACTOR

Above left: Michael reaches for the gun that Clemenza has left for him. Above right: Michael guns down Don Sollozzo and corrupt police chief Captain McCluskey. Bottom left: Coppola directs Sterling Hayden and Al Lettieri. Bottom right: Sterling Hayden in a light-hearted mood during a break from filming.

*Opposite: The aftermath of the assassination. This photograph resembles the work of Weegee (**Arthur Fellig**, 1899-1968), the crime and street photographer famous for his eerie ability to turn up at a crime scene seconds after the authorities.*

Sterling Hayden (1916–1986) was an unlikely film star. Running away to sea at seventeen, he had become a highly respected ship's captain by his early twenties and sailed around the world. He always viewed his career in Hollywood as something of a distraction and simply a way to fund his love of sailing and boats. In contrast, Paramount believed they had found in Hayden the perfect pin-up star and labelled the 6' 5" seaman 'The most beautiful man in movies'. During the war, he left the industry to work as an undercover agent, before enrolling in the Marines (where he signed up as 'John Hamilton' to avoid any unnecessary attention). Hayden emerged from the war with a Silver Star for bravery and a commendation from Yugoslavia's Marshal Tito. Returning to Hollywood in the mid-forties, he again made just enough films to fund his life on the waves. Despite such a nonchalant attitude to the movie industry, Hayden produced an impressive body of work, including arresting turns in *The Asphalt Jungle* (1950), *Johnny Guitar* (1954), *The Killing* (1956), *Dr. Strangelove* (1964), *The Long Goodbye* (1973) and as the crooked cop Captain McCluskey in *The Godfather*.

The character of Apollonia was played by the beautiful Italian actress **Simonetta Stefanelli** (1954–2006). Only sixteen at the time of filming, Stefanelli's innocent beauty captivated audiences and casting directors alike and she went on to star in a number of Italian films. Sadly, she died of cancer in her early fifties and is survived by her husband, the celebrated Italian actor Michele Placido.

Above: Apollonia's beauty hits Michael like a 'thunderbolt'.

Opposite: Michael takes a stroll in the Sicilian countryside with his bodyguards. He has been sent to Sicily by Vito to escape the aftermath of the Sollozzo assassination.

*Above: Michael's bodyguard
protects Apollonia on her
wedding day.*

*Opposite: The wedding
ceremony of Michael and Apollonia.*

Above & Opposite: Michael is too late to save his wife Apollonia, killed by a car bomb intended for him.

RICHARD CONTE, ACTOR

Above: Don Barzini applauding Don Vito's negotiations for peace.

Opposite: Don Barzini at the wedding of Connie Corleone.

Like John Marley, **Richard Conte** (1910–1975) was seriously considered for the role of Don Corleone, but was cast instead as the head of one of the 'five families', Don Barzini.

The son of an Italian-American barber, Conte got his acting break when he was spotted performing by Elia Kazan and John Garfield. Kazan helped him obtain a scholarship to the Neighborhood Playhouse, where he was an outstanding student. His screen debut was in 1939 with *Heaven with a Barbed Wire Fence* and during the early 1940s he became a recognizable face in several war movies. Aside from his role in *The Godfather*, he is best remembered for starring in a number of classic noirs of the forties and fifties, including *Cry of The City* (1948), *Call Northside 777* (1948) and *The Big Combo* (1955).

Above: During filming of the garden scene, Brando was allegedly unhappy with his scripted lines, so Coppola agreed that he would dub fresh dialogue into the scene at a later date. As a consequence, Brando spent the scene telling dirty jokes to Pacino.

Opposite: Vito and his son have a heart-to-heart.

The huge success of *The Godfather* turned many of its cast into multimillion-dollar superstars. At the start of filming, however, most were young unknowns, relatively inexperienced at working on a major movie and nervous at the prospect of working with Hollywood legend Marlon Brando. Brando, however, famously put them all at ease by making jokes and starting a craze for mooning on-set that became a trademark of the shoot, with almost all the male cast and crew joining in.

THE MAN WHO INVENTED LAS VEGAS

Known as 'The man who invented Las Vegas', Moe Green's character was based on real-life mafia boss Benjamin 'Bugsy' Siegel. Siegel opened the first hybrid casino-hotel in the desert of Las Vegas in 1946. Called *The Flamingo* in honour of his girlfriend (it was her nickname), it had financial backing from a number of influential mafiosi. Thus when its grand opening proved a spectacular failure and his backers discovered Siegel had been siphoning funds into his own private Swiss bank account, his fate was sealed. In June 1947, he was killed at home while sitting with his wife and was said to have been shot through the eye (the bullet actually passed through his cheek and nose). Coppola used the same set-up for Moe Green's assassination and it was so effective that this shot has now become a classic of gangster movies.

The actor who played the part of Moe Green had an appropriately criminal past, if popular myth is to be believed. **Alex Rocco** (b.1936) was born Alexander Federico Petricone Jr. and is said to have had connections to the gang that was involved in instigating the notorious Irish Mob Wars in Boston during the 1960s. Whatever the truth about his past out East, when Petricone moved to California, he changed his name and embarked on a highly successful career in Hollywood. Aside from his role in *The Godfather*, Rocco is famous for playing either gangster or comedic roles and has also starred in a number of acclaimed television series, including *The Rockford Files*, *Starsky and Hutch*, *Murder, She Wrote* and *The Simpsons*.

Above: Green is assassinated after Michael discovers he has been stealing money from him.

Opposite: Alex Rocco as Moe Green.

Above left: Michael has Carlo assassinated as revenge for Sonny Corleone's murder. Top right: Actor Gianni Russo had to wear protective leggings during the filming of this scene. Bottom right: Carlo and Connie on their wedding day.

Opposite: Michael watches as the last of his enemies is slain.

Something of a chameleon, **Gianni Russo** (b.1943) has had an interesting and varied career. From a young age, he was a jack of all trades, involved in the nightclub business, real estate and radio. Like Lenny Montana, Russo was a member of the Italian-American Civil Rights League, who got his break in *The Godfather* after helping negotiations between Al Ruddy and the league (see p. 22). After the film showcased Russo's talents as an actor, he went on to star in over forty movies, including *Lepke* (1975), *Any Given Sunday* (1999) and, more recently, *Seabiscuit* (2003). He is also a singer and released an album of songs in 2004.

THE GODFATHER SOUNDTRACK

Nino Rota (1911–1979) was responsible for *The Godfather*'s Academy Award-winning score. Born in Milan, Rota was a child prodigy and works he composed at the age of twelve were performed professionally in Milan and Paris. In his late teens, he won a scholarship to the Curtis Institute of Philadelphia where he studied from 1930–32 before returning to Italy. In 1950, he was appointed the director of the renowned Bari Conservatory and held this position until his death almost thirty years later.

Rota's body of work includes several acclaimed ballets and operas as well as numerous film and theatre scores. He is most famous for composing the music to all of Federico Fellini's films, including *La Dolce Vita* (1960) and *8½* (1963) and for working with other respected directors such as Luchino Visconti, Renato Castellani, René Clément and, of course, Francis Ford Coppola.

Coppola famously involved his family and friends in the filming of *The Godfather* movies and many of them feature as extras. Coppola's father **Carmine Coppola** (1910–1991) in particular contributed to the success of all three films, both on and off set.

A flautist, composer and conductor, Carmine Coppola studied at the Manhattan School of Music and then at Juilliard. He was First Flautist for Radio City Music Hall, the Detroit Symphony and then NBC's Toscanini Orchestra. In the wedding sequence in *The Godfather*, he conducts the orchestra in a piece he composed in honour of the birth of his granddaughter, Sofia. He was even more involved in *The Godfather: Part II*, composing much of the soundtrack for the film, which won an Academy Award (shared with Nino Rota). For *The Godfather: Part III*, he was nominated for an Academy Award for Best Song.

Carmine Coppola went on to work on a number of movies, most notably *Apocalypse Now*, for which he won a Golden Globe for Best Original Score.

Above & Opposite: Brando entertains the cast with his musical talents during breaks in filming.

THE GODFATHER PREMIERE, NEW YORK, MARCH 15 1972

Above: Cast, crew and guests arrive for the premiere of **The Godfather**. *Top, left to right: James Caan, John Marley, Robert Duvall. Middle, left to right: Al Ruddy, Mario Puzo with his wife, Al Pacino with his date Jill Clayburgh. Bottom, left to right: Lenny Montana with his wife, guests of Marlon Brando, Raquel Welch.*

Opposite: Robert Evans with his then wife Ali MacGraw and close friend Henry Kissinger arriving at the Loews theatre for the premiere. All photographs by Fred W. McDarrah.

The release of *The Godfather* was a phenomenon the like of which had never before been witnessed in Hollywood. Paramount's marketing department was keen to exploit the growing hype surrounding the film and a massive, sophisticated campaign was planned with over $1 million spent on advertising. To tie in with the film's premiere, the soundtrack was released; a special paperback edition of the book hit the shelves featuring a thirty-two-page inset of photographs from the film; and an additional one million hardcover copies of the book were published. Announcements were made in magazines nationwide simply stating *The Godfather is Now a Movie* (this popular slogan was also used on one of the advance posters for the film – see p.105).

The film itself premiered on 15 March 1972 at five New York Loews theatres – a radical approach in an industry used to staging cautious, single-cinema premieres. The combined seating of the five theatres was over 4,700, yet even with the maximum number of screenings squeezed into each day the film was in massive over-demand. Average ticket prices were raised from $3 to $4 and the best seats were retailing through ticket touts for as much as $50. When the film was released nationally on 29 March, similar scenes were witnessed across the country. Waiting in line for *The Godfather* became the pop-culture event of 1972.

More than a month after national release, the film continued to gross over $1 million a day and attendance remained at ninety-eight per cent for weeks. By the end of its first run, *The Godfather* had grossed over $81 million domestically and had become the most successful film in history.

1973 ACADEMY AWARDS

Above, left: Coppola with his Oscar. Above middle: Al Ruddy celebrating his Oscar win with Best Actress and Best Supporting Actor winners Liza Minnelli and Joel Grey. Above right: Mario Puzo with his Oscar for Best Writing. (This award was shared with Coppola.)

Opposite: Sacheen Littlefeather surprises Roger Moore and Liv Ullmann at the 1973 Oscars.

The Oscars of 1973 belonged to *The Godfather*. The film was nominated for eleven Academy Awards and won three: Best Picture, Best Writing and Best Actor in a Leading Role. This last was won by Marlon Brando – though he did not collect the award, instead opting to use the most popular night in the entertainment industry's calendar to make a powerful political statement.

Brando was a high-profile, vocal activist for the rights of ethnic minorities throughout his career. His outspoken stance on African-American rights led to his films being effectively banned in many southern states. He was also renowned for his work with the Native-American Civil Rights movement. On winning his Oscar for *The Godfather*, Brando sent a Native-American representative to refuse his award on his behalf, as a protest against the portrayal of Native Americans on television and in Hollywood.

In an interesting footnote, Brando had actually applied to the Academy, only two years previously, for a replacement for his Best Actor Oscar for *On The Waterfront* after it was stolen from his home.

Sacheen Littlefeather (b. Maria Cruz, 1947) had a fifteen-page speech, prepared by Brando, to read at the ceremony. However, after allegedly being threatened by a producer backstage, she spoke for only forty-five seconds, before delivering the full speech to the waiting press pack outside.

*Above: Various prototype designs were considered to head the European poster campaign for the first **Godfather**.*

Opposite: The final version. This illustration of Brando's silhouette has since become one of the most iconic images in cinematic history.
***The Godfather** (1972),*
Original British 41 x 27 in.
(104 x 69 cm).

*Above: **The Godfather: Part II** (1974)*
Original US 41 x 27 in. (104 x 69 cm)
(Advance)

*Opposite: **The Godfather** (1972),*
Original US 41 x 27 in. (104 x 69 cm),
(Advance) .

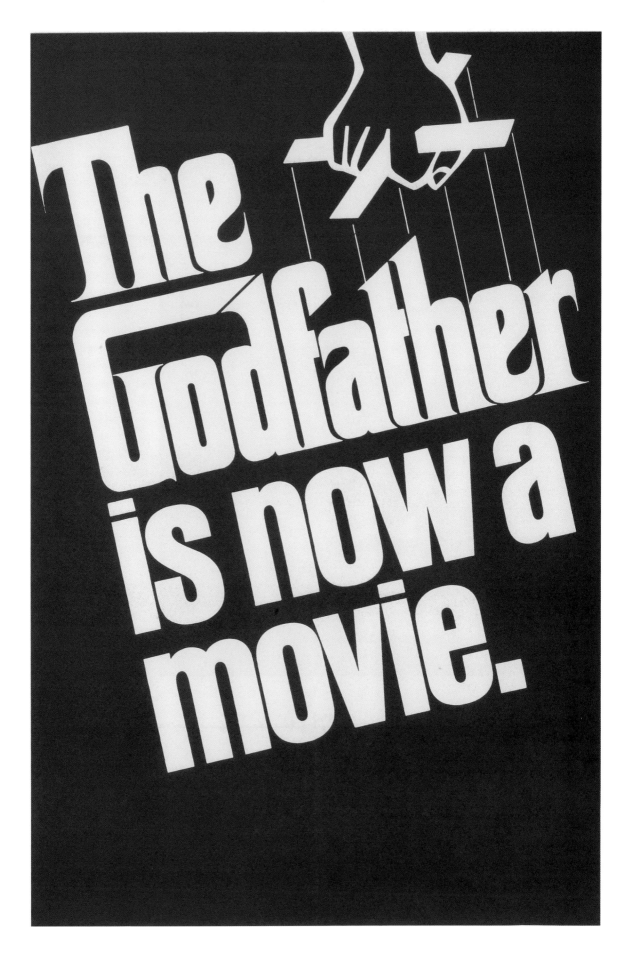

Film amerykański nagrodzony 3 OSKARAMI
OJCIEC CHRZESTNY
Reżyseria: Francis Ford Coppola
W rolach głównych: **Marlon Brando**
Al Pacino   Richard Castellano
James Caan   Produkcja: Alfram

Eastern European film-poster artists are famous for their abstract and conceptual designs. They were often given only a title and brief summary to work from and this factor, combined with a great deal of artistic freedom, has led to the creation of some of the most interesting and unique film posters on record.

Born to Polish émigré parents, **Andrzej Klimowski** (b.1949) studied at St Martin's School of Art in London before moving to the Academy of Fine Art in Warsaw. Several influences are evident in his work, including the traditions of Polish poster art and the paintings of Dalí and other surrealists. His striking and often disturbing images also bear the stamp of an original and creative artist. He is currently head of illustration at the Royal College of Art in London, and the author of several graphic novels.

Tomasz Ruminski (1930–1982) was also a graduate of the Warsaw Academy of Fine Art. He began working in poster design in his mid-twenties and over the next twenty-five years produced an impressive body of work, particularly in the fields of film-, tourism- and advertising posters. His talent won him several awards and his art has been exhibited worldwide. His design for the Polish poster of *The Godfather* remains one of his most recognized works.

*Above: **The Godfather / Ojciec Chrzestny** (1972), Original Polish 33 x 23 in. (84 x 58 cm), Art by Tomasz Ruminski.*

*Opposite: **The Godfather Part II / Ojciec Chrzestny II** (1974), Original Polish 33 x 23 in. (84 x 58 cm), Art by Andrzej Klimowski.*

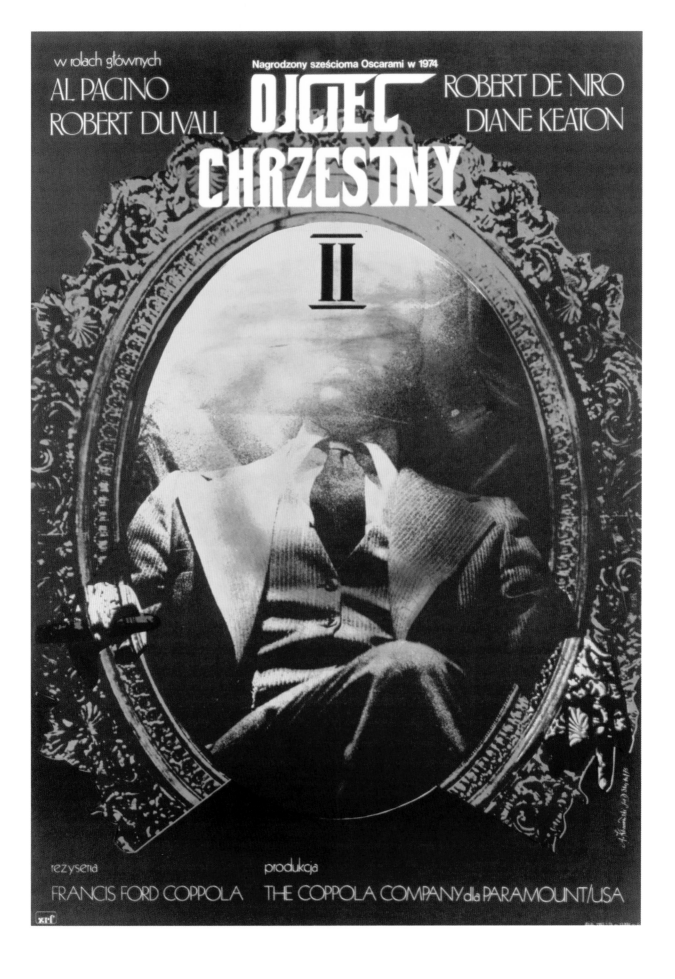

*Above and Opposite: Trade advertisements promoting the release of **The Godfather: Part II**.*

**THE GREAT DYNASTY OF DON VITO CORLEONE
LIVES ON IN HIS SON MICHAEL.
A DYNASTY OF POWER, VIOLENCE, AND CORRUPTION.
A DYNASTY BORN IN SICILY, THAT SPREAD ITS
CORRUPTION TO AMERICA.**

You can kill your enemies.
The enemies fighting you for control of the underworld of Cuba and Las Vegas.

You can kill your friends.
Friends who have done your dirty work for many years.

You can even kill your family.
If they stand in your way or threaten to betray you.

The Godfather PART II
The Most Magnificent Entertainment Of The Year.

Above: The Corleone family pose for a photograph at a party in honour of Anthony's special day in **The Godfather: Part II**. *This photo echoes the famous wedding photograph from the first* **Godfather**.

Opposite: Michael's son Anthony takes his First Communion.

Senator Pat Geary was rumoured to have been based on real-life Nevada Senator Pat McCarran. Although McCarthy is, for most people, the name synonymous with the communist witch-hunts of the 1950s, McCarran was every bit as committed to the cause, and the extent and reach of his power during this bleak period of American history was vast.

G. D. Spradlin (b.1920) had an interesting and varied career before turning his hand to acting. Working first as a lawyer in Venezuela, he then dabbled in independent oil production before experimenting with local politics, campaigning for John F. Kennedy in 1959. It was not until he was into his forties that he joined the Oklahoma Repertory Theatre and discovered a love of acting. Over the next thirty-five years, Spradlin had a prolific career in film and television, starring in over seventy productions before his self-imposed retirement in 1999. His most notable works include *Apocalypse Now* (1979), *The War of the Roses* (1989), *Ed Wood* (1994), *The Long Kiss Goodnight* (1996) and of course his most famous role, as Senator Pat Geary in *The Godfather*.

Above: G. D. Spradlin as Senator Pat Geary.

Opposite: Michael in discussion with Senator Geary.

Richard Bright (1937–2006) played the part of Michael's bodyguard Al Neri in all three *Godfather* movies. Born in Brooklyn, Bright got his break working in live television when he was still only eighteen. A talented screen- and theatre actor, he is most famous for playing 'tough guy' characters. Notable roles include *The Panic in Needle Park* (1971, with *Godfather* co-star Al Pacino), *The Getaway* (1972), *Once Upon a Time in America* (1984) and regular appearances in the hit television series *The Sopranos*.

Above: Richard Bright as Michael's bodyguard Al Neri.

Opposite: Neri stands protectively behind Michael during a business meeting held during Anthony's first Communion.

MICHAEL V. GAZZO, ACTOR

Above: Frankie Pentangeli during the Senate hearing.

Opposite: Michael V. Gazzo as Frankie Pentangeli.

The character of Frankie Pentangeli was rumoured to be based on the infamous mafia informer Joe Valachi. Valachi was the first member of the mafia to publicly admit its existence, and although too low-ranking in the Cosa Nostra chain to implicate any significant leaders, he was a key figure in informing the authorities of the mafia's rituals, codes and practices.

Pentangeli was played by **Michael V. Gazzo** (1923–1995). After serving in the Air Force during the Second World War, Gazzo developed a reputation as a talented playwright. His most famous work, *A Hatful of Rain*, was a massive success on Broadway and was made into a film in 1957, featuring an Oscar-winning turn by Anthony Franciosa. A member of the Actors Studio, Gazzo performed in numerous plays and films, including *The Gang That Couldn't Shoot Straight* (1971) and *Fingers* (1978). He also had a successful career in television, appearing in hit shows such as *Kojak* and *Starsky and Hutch*. He remains most famous, however, for his turn as Pentangeli, which earned him an Academy Award nomination for Best Supporting Actor.

LEE STRASBERG, ACTOR/TEACHER

The character of Hyman Roth was based on real-life Jewish mafia mogul Meyer Lansky. Known as 'The Godfather's Godfather', Lansky was the mob's money man and his power was reportedly vast. Close friends with Lucky Luciano and Bugsy Siegel, he played a key role in developing the National Crime Syndicate (an underworld organisation of business interests). He famously once remarked that the Syndicate was bigger than US Steel – a quote that was written into Roth's lines in *The Godfather*. Lansky also established successful gambling operations in Florida, New Orleans, and pre-Castro Cuba, just as Roth does in the film. Although the FBI failed to find enough evidence to indict Lansky on mafia-related charges, they did manage to catch him on tax evasion and in the early 1970s he fled to Israel for two years before being expelled and forced to return to the States. This too became a key plot twist in *The Godfather*. After the film opened, Lee Strasberg, the actor who played Roth, allegedly received a call from Lansky telling the actor that he had done a great job, but complaining that the character could have been played more sympathetically.

Born Israel Lee Strassberg in a far-flung corner of the Austro-Hungarian Empire (present-day Ukraine), **Lee Strasberg** (1901–1982) moved to America as a child. In 1931 he co-founded the famous Group Theatre, which gave birth to talents such as Elia Kazan and John Garfield, before leaving the Group in 1935 following disagreements over his controversial ideas about acting. In 1950, he became artistic director of the legendary Actors Studio. A hugely influential figure, Strasberg is renowned as one of the founding fathers of method acting. He trained many of the most talented actors of the twentieth century, including James Dean, Al Pacino, Robert De Niro, Ben Gazzara, Eli Wallach, Dustin Hoffman and Marilyn Monroe. (Indeed, he developed such a close friendship with Monroe that she left him a seventy-five per cent share in her estate when she died, including full control of the licensing of her image).

It was Pacino who suggested Lee Strasberg for the role of Hyman Roth, although Coppola and Fred Roos were allegedly too shy to ask him for an interview. Although he had done little actual acting since the thirties, Strasberg was nominated for an Academy Award for the role.

Above: Michael and Hyman Roth take a break during serious discussions to celebrate Roth's birthday in Havana, Cuba.

Opposite: Roth arrives back in the States seconds before being assassinated. This scene is reminiscent of the assassination of Lee Harvey Oswald.

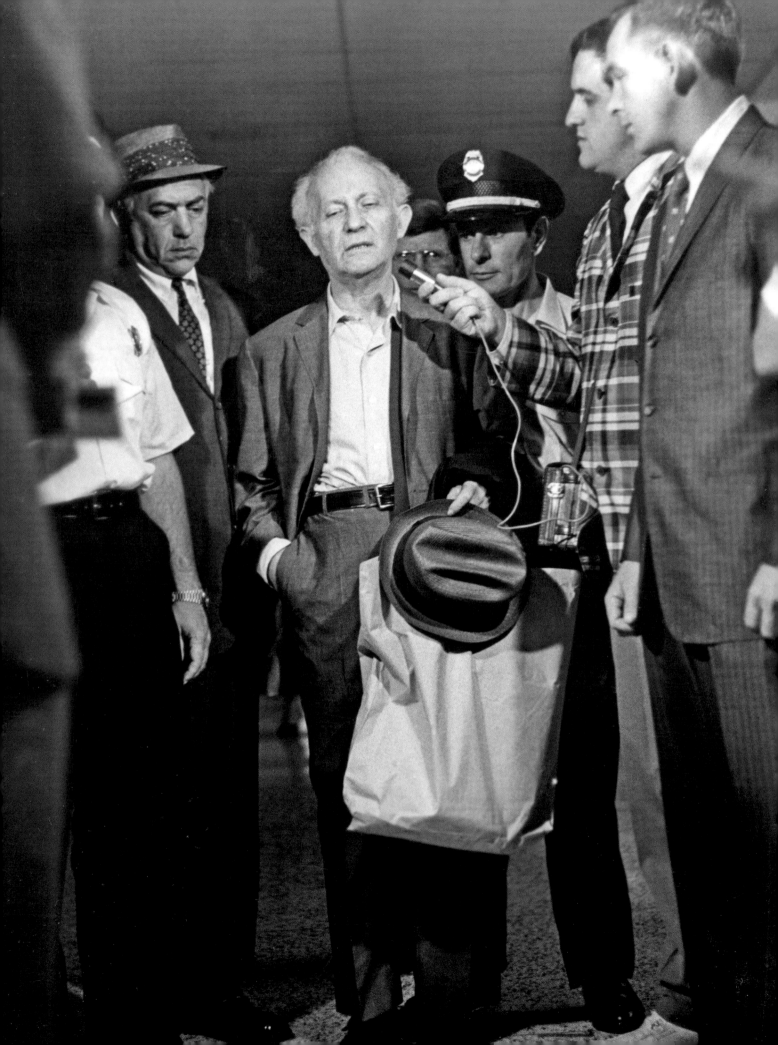

JOHN CAZALE, ACTOR

Top left: Fredo and Michael share a meal together. Top right: Fredo begs for Michael's forgiveness at their mother's funeral. Michael embraces him before ordering his execution. Bottom left: Fredo is embarrassed by his drunken wife at Anthony's party. Bottom right: Fredo weeps after Vito is gunned down.

Opposite: Fredo and Anthony pose for a fishing photograph before Fredo embarks on his fatal boat trip.

John Cazale (1935–1978) managed to escape the endless wrangling and controversy that surrounded the casting of so many in *The Godfather*. Already a respected theatre actor in his early twenties, Cazale was guaranteed the part of Fredo after casting director Fred Roos saw his Obie Award-winning performance in the Israel Horovitz play *Line*.

Born in Boston of Italian-American heritage, Cazale studied drama at Oberlin College and Boston University before moving to New York in the early sixties. Close friends with Al Pacino from a young age, the actors lived together and performed in a number of the same plays, including *The Indian Wants the Bronx* (again by Israel Horovitz), for which both Pacino and Cazale won Obie Awards. Pacino called him his 'acting partner'.

In 1978, Cazale was filming *The Deer Hunter* when he was diagnosed with bone cancer. The studio was keen to recast him, but director Michael Cimino and Cazale's fiancée Meryl Streep (also in the movie), fought his corner tenaciously. By the end of filming, Cazale barely had the strength to make it through his scenes, and tragically died before the premiere.

Cazale starred in five films over the course of his short career, each of which was nominated for an Academy Award for Best Picture (*The Godfather* in 1972, *The Conversation* in 1974, *The Godfather: Part II* in 1974, *Dog Day Afternoon* in 1975 and *The Deer Hunter* in 1978). He is remembered as one of the most talented actors of the 1970s.

DIANE KEATON, ACTRESS

Top left: Kay in bed with Michael in a scene that was cut from the theatrical release. Top right: Kay confronts Michael. Bottom left: Kay getting to grips with the Corleone family during Connie's wedding. Bottom right: Kay, Michael, Mary and Anthony pose for a family portrait at their home in Reno.

Opposite: Diane Keaton on set.

Famous as an Oscar-winning actress, director, producer and fashion icon, **Diane Keaton** (b.1946) earned her reputation in the 1970s. Dropping out of college in the late sixties to study at the Neighborhood Playhouse in New York, she landed a role in the original cast of the Broadway musical *Hair*, becoming notorious during the run for refusing to take off her clothes with the rest of the cast. This reputation worked in her favour and distinguished her from her colleagues. In 1970, she was cast in Woody Allen's Broadway show *Play It Again, Sam* for which she won a Tony Award. (Two years later it was made into a film in which Keaton again starred). Keaton famously became involved with Allen and went on to star in a number of his biggest films of the seventies. Their most successful collaboration was *Annie Hall*, which Allen supposedly wrote specifically about Keaton (her nickname is Annie and her birth name Hall). In addition to her success in these comedic roles, the highlights of Keaton's career have included *The Godfather* trilogy, *Manhattan* (1979), *Reds* (1981) and *Marvin's Room* (1996). Her career is still going strong today. Indeed, by the time she was cast in *The Godfather: Part III*, she commanded a six-figure pay cheque which was second only to Pacino's, a testament to her talent and the reputation she has earned over the course of her career.

AL PACINO, ACTOR

Al Pacino (b.1940) is renowned as one of the foremost actors of his generation and remains one of the most impressive and talented stars working in the industry today. Growing up in New York, Pacino did not have an easy childhood, but from a young age showed a propensity and flair for acting. In his teens, he attended the High School for Performing Arts but dropped out at seventeen in rebellion. Still keen to make a living on the stage, Pacino struggled through a series of dead-end and low-paid jobs to finance his theatre career, where he worked under the stage-name Sonny Scott.

Pacino's breakthrough came in 1966 when he was accepted into the Actors Studio to study under Lee Strasberg. He began to attract attention as one the most talented actors on the circuit, frequently playing brooding, menacing characters. He won an Obie Award for his role in *The Indian Wants the Bronx* for the 67–68 season, shortly followed by a Tony Award for *Does The Tiger Wear a Necktie?*. His film debut was as a bit part in *Me, Natalie* (1969) but it was his soulful turn in *The Panic in Needle Park* (1971) that proved his big break, attracting the attention of Francis Ford Coppola.

The Godfather's success turned Pacino into one of the hottest actors of his generation and his work from this period onwards shows a star at the top of his game. Just as Brando had been, he was nominated for an Academy Award four years running: in 1972 as Best Supporting Actor in *The Godfather*, then as Best Actor for *Serpico* (1973), *The Godfather: Part II* (1974) and *Dog Day Afternoon* (1975). Since the seventies Pacino has been nominated a further four times, winning for *Scent of a Woman* in 1992. His extensive résumé as an actor over the past fifty years includes powerful performances in *Scarface* (1983), *Glengarry Glen Ross* (1992), *Heat* (1995) and most recently *Ocean's Thirteen* (2007).

Top left: Michael and Kay Christmas shopping, shortly before Michael finds out about the assassination attempt on his father's life. Top right: Michael in full army uniform at his sister's wedding. Bottom left: Michael introduces himself to Apollonia. Bottom right: Connie pleads with Michael to forgive Fredo for betraying him.

Opposite: Al Pacino as Michael Corleone.

THE GODFATHER ON TELEVISION

In 1974, NBC paid Paramount $10 million for the TV rights for a single showing of *The Godfather*, to be shown over two consecutive nights. This was the highest price ever paid for such a transmission, and advertisers were charged over $250,000 for a minute of airtime during the screening. It became the most watched film in television history to that date.

In 1977, NBC again secured a deal for a single, consecutive-night showing of *The Godfather* and *The Godfather: Part II*. The contract rested on the stipulation that Coppola completely re-edit the films for the screening. Forced home from filming *Apocalypse Now* after a typhoon destroyed the set, Coppola began to tackle the project with close childhood friend and editor of *Apocalypse Now*, Brian Malkin. Starting afresh with the complete uncut footage from both films, their starting point was to piece together all the scenes in chronological order for simplicity, with a view to reworking it once it was organized. However, when the reels of film were thus arranged, they had a beautiful continuity and clarity.

Having thus decided on a format, the slow process of re-editing began. By now, Coppola had returned to the Philippines and the two friends communicated by fax, each working on the project from their respective corners of the world. NBC needed some of the more offensive elements removed, so certain scenes were shortened and dialogue reworked. Coppola even employed sound crews to re-record several of the actors's voices, including Robert De Niro, Robert Duvall and Lee Strasberg, and then had this dubbed over the original script. Scenes cut from the original were re-inserted, new music was scored and subtitles were added for the Sicilian scenes. The finished product included over fifty-seven minutes of extra footage and ran at seven hours and fourteen minutes (which meant over nine hours of television, once commercials were inserted). It was officially credited as *Mario Puzo's The Godfather: The Complete Saga for Television* (which later became the video release: *The Godfather: The Complete Epic, 1902–1959*).

The screening again broke all previous records. Shown on four consecutive nights in November 1977, the country ground to a halt and by the last night of the screening, forty-three per cent of the television-watching public were tuned into *The Godfather*.

Perhaps most famous from his time at *Mad* magazine, **Jack Davis** (b.1924) is one of the most influential and renowned American cartoonists of the twentieth century. Born in Atlanta, Davis attended the Art Student's League of New York before beginning freelance work in the late 1940s. His versatility, speed and skill as a caricaturist, combined with his frenetic, unique style attracted EC Comics and he began freelancing for them in 1950. Two years later, when *Mad* was released, Davis became a staple on the publication and over the next two decades, his reputation soared.

Aside from his work with EC Comics, Davis has illustrated book jackets, record sleeves and movie posters and has worked on almost every major magazine, from *Time* to *TV Guide*. During the seventies he was briefly listed as the highest paid illustrator in the world as a result of the body of advertising work he was producing for leading companies. Exhibitions of Davis's work have been mounted worldwide and he has won a series of awards including the Lifetime Achievement Award from the National Cartoonist Society in 1996, being inducted into the Comic Book Hall of Fame in 2003 and the Society of Illustrators Hall of Fame in 2005.

*Opposite: **TV Guide**, November 16-22, 1974. Cover art by Jack Davis.*

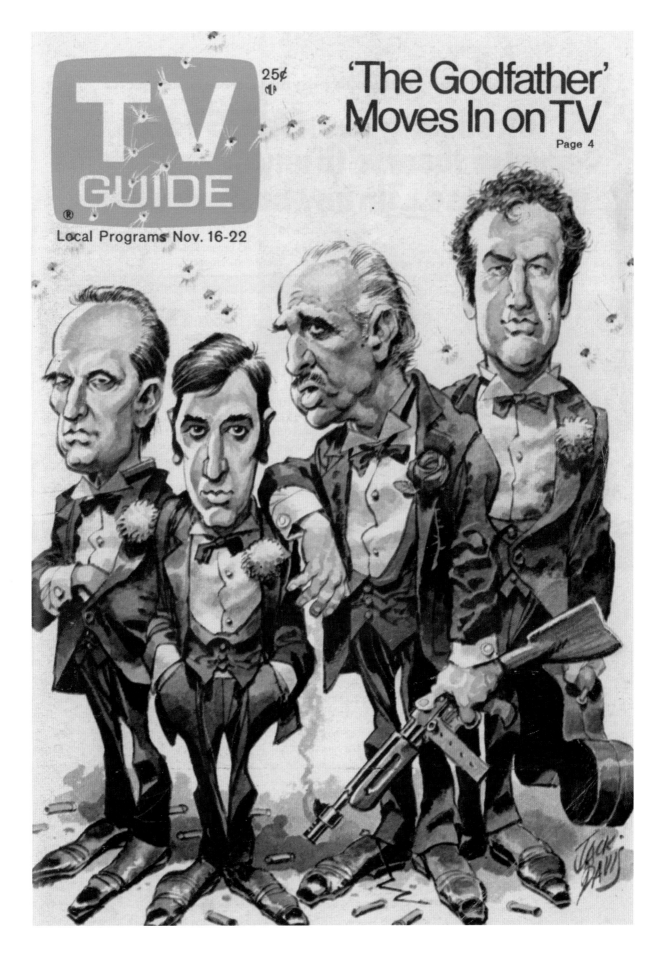

THE MAKING OF THE GODFATHER: PART III

Paramount had always been keen to make a third *Godfather* film, considering the astounding success of the first two movies. Between 1974 and 1989, twelve people worked on the script and numerous directors were considered, including Michael Mann, Warren Beatty and Martin Scorsese. Despite the studio's attempts at persuasion, Coppola was fiercely against making it, stating he would never return for a third film and would only ever make it if it was a farce in the style of Mel Brooks. However, the 1980s saw something of a reversal in Coppola's good fortune. Several box-office failures, combined with an expensive law suit, had left him heavily in debt and this allegedly proved the decisive factor in changing his mind with regards to the *Godfather* project.

Coppola came on board on the stipulation that he would have complete control over the script and that he would receive $6 million plus fifteen per cent of the film's gross takings. He also wanted six months to write and develop the script. Paramount, however, wanted the movie rushed through for a Christmas 1990 release, and so he was ultimately only given six weeks. The result was a film that Coppola was never happy with and which received reviews that were disappointing compared with the lavish critical success of the first two movies. However, viewed on its own merits, the film was still a great success and was nominated for seven Academy Awards including Best Picture, Best Director and Best Actor.

Above: Family and friends pose for a photograph during the party to celebrate Michael's papal honour.

Opposite: Archbishop Gilday presents Michael with his medal.

THE CASTING OF VINCENT MANCINI

Above: Actors considered for the role of Vincent Mancini. Clockwise from top left: Alec Baldwin, Matt Dillon, Vincent Spano, Val Kilmer, Charlie Sheen and Nicholas Cage. All photographs circa 1990.

Opposite: Andy Garcia as Vincent.

Just as the character of Michael had been one of the most sought-after roles of the seventies, so too was that of Vincent Mancini in *The Godfather: Part III*. Several actors were considered for the role, including Val Kilmer, Vincent Spano, Alec Baldwin, Matt Dillon, Nicholas Cage (who is Coppola's nephew) and Charlie Sheen (whose father Martin had been one of the original actors considered to play Michael). The young actor who finally secured the part was Andy Garcia.

THE CASTING OF MARY CORLEONE

*Above: Actresses considered
for the role of Mary Corleone. Top
left: Winona Ryder, bottom left:
Madonna. Right: Julia Roberts.*

*Opposite: Sofia Coppola as
Mary Corleone.*

Many actresses were in the running for the part of Michael's daughter Mary. Julia Roberts was allegedly the studio's first choice but was already committed to another project. Madonna was another strong favourite, but the role was ultimately given to Winona Ryder, then at the pinnacle of her career. Having made five films in two years, however, she suddenly withdrew from *The Godfather* project citing exhaustion. Running out of time and money to find a new female star, Coppola turned to his own daughter Sofia.

SOFIA COPPOLA, ACTRESS/DIRECTOR

Top left: Mary dances with Michael at the party to celebrate his receiving the medal of the Order of St. Sebastian from the Vatican. Top right: Mary and Vincent's relationship develops. Bottom left: Michael with his daughter. Bottom right: Mary is assassinated.

Opposite: Mary and Vincent at the opera in Sicily.

Francis Ford Coppola's daughter **Sofia Coppola** (b.1971) had had bit parts in the first two *Godfather* films, most notably as the baby Anthony christened at the end of *The Godfather*. *The Godfather: Part III*, however, was the first real showcase of her talents as an actress. Though many critics were hard on her performance in the film, Coppola has gone on to become one of the most gifted and creative young writer-directors in Hollywood. Her three major directorial works to date, *The Virgin Suicides* (1999), *Lost in Translation* (2003) and *Marie Antoinette* (2006) are all critically acclaimed dramas. For *Lost in Translation*, Coppola won the Academy Award for Best Original Screenplay and was nominated for Best Picture and Best Director. Indeed, she was the first American woman (and only the third woman at all) ever to be nominated for an Oscar for Best Director.

ANDY GARCIA, ACTOR

Born Andres Arturo Garcia Menendez in Havana, **Andy Garcia** (b.1956) was five years old when Castro came to power, causing his family to flee to the United States. Although initially struggling to make ends meet, his father (who had been a lawyer in Cuba) developed a multi-million-dollar fragrance company and the family built a new life for themselves in Miami.

Garcia was a gifted sportsman, but following a serious illness in his final year of high school, he was forced to take a prolonged period of rest and instead turned to drama. Discovering a real passion and talent for the art, he went on to study acting at Florida International University. He got his first break in his mid-twenties on the hit show *Hill Street Blues* and this secured him one of his first film roles as a drug dealer in *8 Million Ways To Die* (1986). On seeing his powerful performance, Brian de Palma offered him a role in his upcoming picture, *The Untouchables* (1987). This film showcased the depth of his abilities and solidified his reputation as one of the rising stars of his generation.

Famous for religiously guarding his privacy, Garcia chooses his film roles carefully, working only on projects in which he really believes. In addition to *The Untouchables* and *The Godfather: Part III*, his most notable roles include *Black Rain* (1989), *Internal Affairs* (1990) and *Ocean's Eleven* (2001). In 2005, he directed and starred in *Lost City*. A personal project of Garcia's, it tells the story of a family caught up in the violence of the Cuban revolution and forced to flee their own country for America.

Top left: Coppola directs Garcia on set. Top right: Vincent guns down Joey Zasa. Bottom: Vincent supports Michael as he tells the heads of the families he is buying them out.

Opposite: Andy Garcia as Vincent on location in Italy.

JOE MANTEGNA, ACTOR

The character of Joey Zasa is said to have been based on real-life mobster boss John Gotti, who was renowned for his flashy dress sense – although in *The Godfather: Part III*, Zasa fails to kill Michael, whereas Gotti famously succeeded in assassinating his boss, Paul Castellano, in an orchestrated hit.

The Italian-American **Joe Mantegna** (b.1947) was born and raised in Chicago and is a highly respected actor. His body of stage- and screen work over the last few decades is impressive: in the late seventies he won a Tony Award for the stage play of *Glengarry Glen Ross*; in 1988, he won Best Actor at the Venice Film Festival for *Things Change*; and in 2004, he was given a Lifetime Achievement Award by the Los Angeles Italian Film Festival. *Things Change* was one of three films Mantegna collaborated on with director David Mamet. Alongside *House of Games* (1987) and *Homicide* (1991), this trilogy includes some of Mantegna's most powerful performances. Mantegna is still actively involved in theatre and film today, and is also famous as the voice of 'Fat Tony' in *The Simpsons*.

Above top: Joey Zasa is gunned down by Vincent. Above bottom: Copola directs Joe Mantegna on set.

Opposite: Joe Mantegna as Joey Zasa.

Above: Michael during negotiations with the Vatican.

Opposite: George Hamilton as consigliere B.J. Harrison.

The role of consigliere B.J. Harrison was played by **George Hamilton** (b.1939). Having taken up acting in high school, Hamilton was one of the last stars ever contracted by MGM, appearing in such hits as *Home From the Hill* (1960) and *Two Weeks In Another Town* (1962). He has had a long and successful career in television and film, with his most recent work including Woody Allen's *Hollywood Ending* (2002).

ELI WALLACH, ACTOR

Above top: Vincent pays his respects to the traitor Don Altobello. Above bottom: Connie hands Altobello the poisoned cannoli at the opera.

Opposite: Eli Wallach as Don Altobello.

Eli Wallach (b.1915) is one of Hollywood's greatest and longest-serving character actors. Still working after more than fifty years in the business, he is that rare commodity – an actor who has continued to be offered interesting roles in his later years, such as that of Don Altobello in *The Godfather: Part III*.

Born and raised in New York, Wallach was trained in the method school of acting at the famous Actors Studio and Neighborhood Playhouse. He took a break from the industry to fight in the Second World War, but returned to the stage and debuted on Broadway in 1945. In 1951 he won a Tony Award for his performance in Tennessee Williams's *The Rose Tattoo*, and five years later made his screen debut with another Williams play, *Baby Doll*. From such auspicious beginnings, he has gone on to star in well over a hundred films, most notably *The Magnificent Seven* (1960), *The Misfits* (1961) and as Tuco (the Ugly) in Sergio Leone's *The Good, The Bad and The Ugly* (1966). His body of television work is also impressive and includes *Kojak, Alfred Hitchcock Presents, Naked City* and *Law & Order*.

Previous page: Michael and Vincent
share an intimate conversation.
Above: Coppola directs Pacino.
A picture of Marlon Brando as
Vito Corleone hangs on the
wall behind them.

Opposite: Al Neri kisses Vincent's
hand, symbolising his allegiance to
the new head of the family.

DEAN TAVOULARIS, PRODUCTION DESIGNER

Above: Coppola and Dean Tavoularis.

Opposite: The talented opera singer Frank D'Ambrosio as Anthony Corleone.

Production designer **Dean Tavoularis** (b.1932) studied architecture and painting before landing his first job as a storyboard artist at Disney. In 1967, he became artistic director on *Bonnie and Clyde*, and it was his talented work on this film that first attracted Coppola's attention. *The Godfather* saw the start of a great collaboration between the designer and director. Tavoularis went on to work on several of Coppola's films, including *The Conversation* and *Apocalypse Now*, for which he created a huge, sprawling lost city in the jungle. It was this remarkable ability to transform any space into magnificent and complex sets that earned him the nickname 'The Magician', and led to him becoming one of the most sought after names in the business. Tavoularis worked on all three *Godfather* movies, winning an Academy Award for his work on *Part II*.

INDEX

Opposite: Robert De Niro as Vito Corleone in Little Italy.

Overleaf: Coppola examines a strip of film during the editing of **The Godfather: Part II**.